Possessions

Possessions

A Memoir of Transformation in an Era of Precarity

Davina Quinlivan

Illustrations by James Roberts

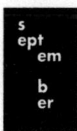

First published in the United Kingdom by September in 2026

September, an imprint of Duckworth Books Ltd
1 Golden Court, Richmond, TW9 1EU, United Kingdom
www.septemberpublishing.org

A catalogue record for this book is available from the British Library

Book design and typesetting by Danny Lyle

Printed and bound in Great Britain by CPI Books

The authorised representative in the EEA is Easy Access System
Europe, Mustamäe tee 50, 10621 Tallinn, Estonia.

1

Hardback ISBN: 9780715656044
eISBN: 9780715656051

For All Those Who Were Present

Author's note

This is a work of memoir and of imagination. For privacy purposes I have changed identifying characteristics of individuals and places, and for narrative purposes I have on occasion combined people and altered the chronology. Some conversations have been recreated from memory and others are entirely imagined.

Contents

My upside-down feet touched the sky and my hair, a curtain of black waves, was on fire. All was burning and I could not catch my breath. Yet, I was calm. The stars had enveloped my body and my hands seemed to gently, so gently, crack open the earth where lava overflowed and spluttered. Streaks of light. An unbinding, quick as the foot of a hare. Brittle, sulphurous heat snaked between my fingers and I could smell the smoke of a hundred burning teak trees. My thoughts gathered and grew into spirals of movement in the air.

A vital throng. A tiny heartbeat. Another and then another.

I was the twitching robin in the tree, the curve of the riverbank, the weight of water.

I floated out of my skin in slow motion, utterances leaving me in a reverse chord. I wore the world lightly.

The last breath I took sounded like a sigh. At least, that was what I told myself. Really, it was a word, which curled persistently over the stone of my stiffening tongue. Three syllables:

Pos-ses-sion

But I was not the one being possessed. I had been consumed so many times before and now it was my turn to devour everything. I made more space inside myself so that I could savour every bite.

I stretched out my hands and raised my palms to the sky, to the air, to the robin in the tree.

1
Academic Barbie

I wanted to be like Carol Vorderman when I was a teenager, but I could never do the maths equations. I wanted the tousled, blonde hair of Drew Barrymore and the eyes of Jennifer Lopez. A friend once told me to do it: *Just dye your hair, get it out of your system.* Straightening my hair, I burned myself. I burned my forehead too, with curling tongs, and pinched my eyelids with eyelash curlers. Deep down, I knew blonde hair would never suit me, so I flung a black shawl around my shoulders, à la Lopez in one of her music videos, and I danced the flamenco.

Before others tried to change me, I tried to change myself. Instinctively, I developed a habit, perfecting the art of self-imposed conditioning, preparation for the more violent and pernicious forms of possession that were to come. And they were coming, thick and fast. All I had to do was wait.

POSSESSIONS

It starts when someone takes a photograph of you, but first let's begin with more primitive portraits like a drawing. A loner at school once painted a life-size portrait of me with my girl gang on the walls of the art room when no one was looking. He stole poster paint and large sheets of coloured sugar paper, taping them to the windows. In an act of equal parts vandalism and boredom, he painted white trainers and high ponytails, curvy bodies stuck perpetually in some sort of moody stance. A mural that had made giants of us all. He had drawn me pretty, but in a pigment that resembled Marge Simpson. It was a compliment, in a way, and then not, obviously. One of my friends caught him by the collar and squared up to him until he apologised.

Elsewhere, I was photographed by family members with my nan's Chinese fan and a sparkly hat like the one Kylie Minogue wore on the cover of her *Enjoy Yourself* album. I never forgot the photography teacher who said I had *interesting features*. I didn't know what that meant. A few years later, I bought a Chinese mask, a theatrical figurehead in gold and crimson, on a whim for a friend's birthday. *It's just like you*, they said. After that, I didn't like my photograph being taken unless I trusted the person with the camera. I let my fringe grow long until it covered half my face. Even now I still feel vulnerable if my hair isn't a thick blanket I can hide behind.

Sometimes, if you watch closely, you can see me pulling at it while I'm talking, comforted by these strands of hair, puffing them up to ensure they generate their imaginary protection.

We were taught at school about Native American Indians and how they were fearful of photography, because the camera would steal their 'soul', but that's an oversimplification of the facts. It was the camera's intrusion and visual power that frightened them the most, a piece of technology which held the potential to make a spectacle of their identity and culture. The camera was another tool of colonisation, because the photographs possessed them and controlled the narrative. Taking back the story, that's the tricky part. From a young age, I learned that I liked writing about images, art, representation, but I did not like being the image itself. I slunk away from any position that might have afforded me. In my late teens, I wore a heavy coat to cover my body and pulled my hair around my face (*Don't you want to take that off? No, no, I'm fine, really…*).

I once did some work experience at a fashion magazine, where I was the anonymous tester for a new brand of mascara. They printed a tiny picture of my teenage face somewhere towards the back of the magazine, while the rest of the pages contained models who gazed vacantly at me from their milky white forms and long legs. I folded back the little headshot of me, embarrassed of myself. I wanted other people's bodies before anything else, but it wasn't just the idea of having a different body that I clung to; it was also about how that body existed in space and time. My timelines were skewered – I felt increasingly out of time and out of place, but I didn't know why.

I was living in a strange netherworld my parents had constructed for me out of the ruins of their respective childhoods, almost entirely obliterated by World War II. They poured these experiences into me, but I had no way of making sense of them. Lo and behold, I developed a passionate fixation with the American TV show *Quantum Leap* in which Sam, a scientist from the future, is trapped in time, his consciousness 'leaping' from one body to the next within his own timeline in order to 'put right what once went wrong'. I still don't understand why no one ever explained where Sam's corporeal existence went while he occupied other people's bodies. Did he completely vanish, or did he just become a fugitive presence? I guess we'll never know.

Lovely Sam never chose to become a 'leaper'; he was just propelled backwards in time when his experiment went wrong. Only now I understand why I couldn't get enough of Sam's sci-fi adventures. I never chose to live my life within a cycle of collective fate which, in actuality, extended well beyond my own timeline, going all the way back to the early days of the British Empire.

I've never stopped feeling like it's my job to put right everything that went wrong. Part of me still wants to swap places with my parents and erase their memories of war. In an alternative reality, I could restore their innocence. I could give them back the childhoods they deserved. Instead of my presence, there would just be a hole in time where I once existed, and perhaps that incision in history would simply fill up with love. Perhaps, that feeling of love could be just like the shining light of a star exploding and dying in some far-off galaxy. Their happiness in exchange for the universe which made me flesh and bone. I won't lie about that, it's just how I feel. I wish I never saw that look in their eyes, which told me something was wrong and will always be wrong; that look, which revealed to me the missing parts of them that I shall never be able to retrieve. Even as I child, I felt their pain as if it were my own.

I didn't have many dolls as a child, but I was given a hospital Barbie set, which I employed in order to 'direct' my own episodes of TV shows like *Baywatch* or *Neighbours*. During one particular episode of *Baywatch*, a bikini-clad lifeguard had her leg attacked by a shark. I went straight up to my bedroom, organising the dolls so that I could explore that moment in close-up detail. How could such perfection unravel so quickly? Surely, her leg would be saved and, in the following episode, it was. In the future, I'm the director of that memory and I still see myself with my little black bowl cut, holding the dolls by their ridiculously long plastic legs, perched by the powder blue, miniature hospital bed. Maybe I sensed a shark was after me too – the shark under my bed, which we can also call by its true name: inferiority.

What is it like to want a body when it's not your own? From a young age, I had been told I was *unusual, striking* or, in less kindly terms, I had a *hard face, very dark hair resembling a wig, pale skin*, etc.… As I grew older, I became the screen for other people's projections, dreams of otherness, strangeness. It didn't matter what I said or did, because I became a sign, an open symbol that called to them, called to them to name me and to give me meaning while my mouth said nothing. The hieroglyph. Shy, quiet girl.

I was also possessed by the images I saw on the television. I was bitterly disappointed with the fact that I didn't look anything like Kelly from *Saved by the Bell* or the freckled, blue-eyed girl who played the lead in *Sabrina the Teenage Witch*. I saw parts of myself in Mayim Bialik's precocious teen from *Blossom* or Claire Danes's melancholic, grungy

Angela in *My So-Called Life*, but this didn't prevent me from wanting to be thinner, so I timed myself jogging on the spot, stretching and touching my toes as *Now That's What I Call Music 1993* played on my Sony stereo. As I grew thinner, people still tried to claim my body, telling me I looked like this person or that person, but it always had to be someone. They just wouldn't let me be me.

While I was so focused on changing the way I looked, they were taking my head off and claiming my body for themselves. They named me *Snow White, Pocahontas, Titania*, even one of Paul Gauguin's *mournful Tahitian girls*, which, by the way, was a throw-away comment made by an old Oxbridge graduate with his own experimental jazz ensemble. I felt myself being fixed into the pages of a book I hadn't written. They always looked at me as if they were flattening me out and gluing me into a scrapbook. Over time, I had a feeling they weren't just fastening me to the pages of some mythical book, but also cutting off my head with scissors, replacing it with their own. *Snip. Snip. Snip.* My head drifted off from the pages and floated to the floor as they cut me out. I tried to glue myself back, but once you cut something off, you can always see the breakage lines and these can never be smoothly reclaimed.

My hieroglyph features brand me as 'exotic', a word that is used often by men to describe how I look. It has a dehumanising quality, that word. To call someone exotic is to 'other' them, to get out the scissors so that you can construct your own fantasies, which, according to Freud, perfectly riffs off the fact that the patriarchy has historically perceived women as objects to be possessed. If you are already branded as other, mysterious and foreign, then you are condemned to a lifetime of being stuck between the scissors.

Around the age of thirteen, I had my backside caressed while standing in an aisle in a grocery store in Southall (the first of many times during my youth) and then, while walking home from school with a group of friends, I was flashed at by a white male in his sixties. One of my friends had made a conscious effort to report this incident to the police and the next day a policewoman rocked up at my house, while my father paced the hallway in our 1930s semi, helpless and alarmed. These experiences probably had less to do with my face and more to do with my age. Girls endure these things. Odd-shaped feelings poured into me and I drank them in, believing that was what it was like to be desired.

By nineteen, I thought I could handle the exotic thing and foolishly decided to use it to get what I wanted.[1] I pushed the 'real me' under the carpet and played dress-up to capture what I thought was an attractive and otherwise unattainable prize from the middle-class, bohemian world I longed to be part of.

I became someone else's fantasy – plainly a 'Tahitian girl' or 'Pocahontas' – and it ended with me standing outside in the rain in Twickenham waiting for a Welsh actor with an elegant face to open the door, but he never did, pathetically signing off via text message (received on my cobalt blue 'Pay As You Go' Nokia 5110): *You're wonderfully gorgeous and talented but…* Alas, he was holding up the pair of scissors I had willingly passed to him on a plate, and on their tapered blades I saw reflected the glow of the white-washed walls of his Victorian house and my severed head, abandoned on the steps outside.

Aside from the threat of scissors, I've always felt as if my head was a bit wobbly, under pressure to float off into the ether. I fear I owe this feeling to my ancestry. I descend from a few Burmese tribes including the Padaungs. *Padaung* is a word that literally translates as 'long neck'. From around the age of six, heavy brass coils are attached to the necks of young girls, giving them the illusion of a swan's physiognomy. The coils symbolise wealth, status and beauty, and the girls willingly accept this barbarism, just like those that were subjected to the ancient Chinese tradition of foot binding, whereby feet are painfully contorted into fetishised 'lotus' shapes. There is an entry in the *Guinness Book of Records* that refers to a Padaung tribeswoman's neck measuring forty centimetres. The coils put pressure around the collarbone and the ribs.

One by one, the coils form a brace of sorts, which gradually pushes the chin upwards and everything else downwards, permanently weakening the neck muscles. Heads seem to rise unnaturally high above the body. Imagine that.

I don't really need anyone to worry about my head being cut off my body, *snip-snip*, because some of my ancestors were halfway there already. Apparently, the coils don't hurt, but it's funny, isn't it, how we can become conditioned to ignore pain? The journalist and colonial administrator J. G. Scott writes about the Padaung women's voices emanating from their bodies as if they were *speaking from the bottom of a well*. Sometimes I wonder if the spirits of my female ancestors live on, quite literally, inside of me, wearing their coils with pride as they watch me go about my daily life. Perhaps this is why everything to me is such a fucking pain in the neck.

Which possessions came before me, drenching my bones? Which ones did I accept, and which ones did I resist? My Burmese paternal grandmother, Maggie, had a stroke long before I was able to talk, so she couldn't impart any knowledge or wisdom to her youngest granddaughter. In her wheelchair, in which she remained until her death in 1993 when I was twelve, she would hold my hands, press her thumbs against my cheeks and smile the widest of smiles. Her eyes still twinkled when I brushed her short, silver hair with her plastic comb. Her voice only existed as a set of extremely slurred and incomprehensible moans, *ooohs* and *aahhhs*. Severe strokes affect the brain's ability to control speech muscles, leading to aphasia. Aphasia doesn't make a person less expressive or able to feel emotion; it simply means that they struggle to linguistically communicate.

When Maggie spoke, it didn't sound like she was speaking from the bottom of a well, like our ancestors. She sounded more like a damaged cassette tape, groaning and sighing, eyes closed in frustration as she tried to exhale the words. She was in her body, but trapped inside it without a voice. Yet she seemed content whenever I was around her. I was never afraid of the weird, bagpipe-like noises her body made. To me, she was just a big smiling head. The stroke had severed Maggie from her body while her mind still whirred around. It makes sense to me how much she enjoyed the Saturday boxing matches on the telly. Maybe television allowed her to jump from her paralysed body into theirs, just for a moment. *KAPOW–KABOOM–WHACK!* Perhaps she jumped into my body from time to time, as I ran up and down the stairs in her home, tore foil wrappers from chocolate bars and jumped on her single bed. Come to think of it, her smile was probably a bit maniacal, because she held the knowledge we were both participating in some sort of strange, cosmic dance.

Snip, snip, snip, the idea of heads without bodies usually serves as a metaphor, one way or another, for a removal of power, of order. A 'headless state' is a country without a ruling system. This is also, of course, literal in the case of history, as simple as seeing the Queen's head on a stamp (I know we have a king now, but it's the idea of the Queen's head that I've carried around with me for four decades). As a child, I had once seen Anne Boleyn's head roll off into a straw-lined basket in one of those films about Henry VIII (sound effect: the slicing of a fat cabbage falling into a deep, wicker bowl).

Then, there is the frequent symbolism of beheadings when it comes to saints and the common hagiographical motif associated with what is broadly known as the Celtic 'cult of the head', whose devotion was, specifically, to the idea of the head as 'the seat of the soul'. Martyred by beheading, these cephalophoric saints are usually depicted in art, sculpture or tapestries, and so on, carrying their own head.

The semi-rural city near where I live now, in the west of England, has its own headless patron saint whose martyrdom dates back to CE 740. The patron saint of my home city, Saint Sidwella, was a virtuous Romanised Christian girl whose story ends in her beheading in a cornfield, much like the one I stare out at now from my bedroom window. After visiting the sick, Sidwella had been kneeling in prayer when a pair of corn reapers, employed by her jealous pagan stepmother, approached with a scythe. For three nights, the spot where her head had fallen was illuminated by a 'heavenly shaft of light', or so the scriptures say. On the fourth night, Sidwella was seen walking in the fields with her head miraculously reattached to her body. Every time I look out to the fields beyond my bedroom window, I think of Sidwella alone out there.

Unlike my inconceivably long-necked Padaung ancestors whose voices, as Scott had it, sounded as if they were disappearing down a well, the spot where Sidwella's head had lain brought forth a sacred well, before the rest of her, I suppose, walked off into the fields and vanished into thin air. Except, Sidwella didn't walk off into nothingness, because she is a saint. Sidwella's story ends with her striding towards a site where her martyrdom would ensure the founding of a church and thus preserve Christianity. Indeed, a church of early Anglo-Saxon origin – St Sidwell's – still stands on the consecrated ground where she came to rest.

Most peculiarly, action was taken by Tesco in the 1960s to commission a giant five- or six-metre-tall bas-relief dedicated to Sidwella's memory. Local art teacher Frederick Irving moulded Sidwella's face from the casting of a young life model and art student called Meg Compton. It's hard not to imagine Meg as an arty hippy with a penchant for Joni Mitchell. It was Meg's clever hands which made Sidwella's waist-length, corn-coloured plaits, lending her, or at least this version of the saint, an air of flower power, Mitchell-esque charm. I often catch myself glancing up at that mural where Tesco once was, now long gone and replaced with, of all things, an NHS walk-in centre. It remains unclear if that specific incarnation of this building pays tribute to Sidwella's healing powers, or if the supermarket chain was in any way intent on establishing itself, by way of association, as part of a divine order of local sanctity. And so it is that the image of a young art student's face, with her large, exaggerated eyelids closed shut in prayer, conflates with the memory of a saint.

While the Celtic cult of the head believed in the soul as something that resides within the head of the body, René Descartes wrote about the dualism of the mind and body, joined but also distinct in their nature and substance. This theory of dualism is what gave the age of Enlightenment an empowered vision of itself. Yet, the more the intellect developed, the more civilised humanity became, and that also put us at a very polite remove from all earthly sensations. Knowledge, intellect, made us more than our bodies, more than flesh. It was an idea that struck me as a way to escape.

If I could be clever enough and learn the rules of that cleverness and how it operated, then I would not have the problem of my body. Or so it seemed.

I followed the books. Speaking in tongues, I sung from the academia-themed gospel sheet I was handed and the chorus anointed me. I renounced the language I was born with; I spoke in pure, ringing syllables and clipped, smooth sounds. I felt myself separate into two parts: the uneducated girl with the accented hieroglyph bones and the buttoned-up academic; the bearer of an accepted, normative form of knowledge and its linguistic power. I held the two things inside of me as different as night and day, wrong and right, good and bad, ugly and beautiful, ignorant and brilliant. Nothing was on the border of these feelings, or at least if there was any kind of border, it was something I just ignored, like damp socks falling down the back of a radiator.

I'm acutely aware of the fact that, like Sam from *Quantum Leap*, a version of myself has been sacrificed in order to put right all the 'wrongs'. I've assimilated in ways my parents could only ever dream of. I changed myself so that these historic, inherited wounds of colonialism and racism could heal through my assimilation and subservience. Part of myself retreated and waited in the shadows, while this other thing spoke at academic conferences, pointed at screens, paused and breathed in ways that were redolent of an intellectual's gait, a body performing the will of the mind. The rejected, other parts of myself hung their heads and their hair fell in waves of dark matter. Their multiple bodies shrunk to the size of a betel nut. Imagine all those betel nuts bouncing around. My smallest selves, my Asian and East Asian ancestors, bit their tiny tongues, while my colonial ancestors of European (French, Scottish, Irish, German) origin trimmed my vowels and invisibly tended to my self-doubting thoughts as if shaping topiaries with silver secateurs. *Snip. Snip. Snip.* This is how I began to desire knowledge more than other people's body parts.

As I grew older, I felt a second, synthesised skin clothe my naked hieroglyph bones. I became an academic in black dresses and black tights, quoting artists and philosophers like an incantation, while ancient words in my ancestral languages were sublimated or gagged, any sign of them willingly absented, exiled. I shoved a black pashmina down their many throats. To appease my ancestors, should they come after me, I decorated my neck with jade, whose symbolism in Burmese culture represents righteousness and virtue. Occasionally, my body yearned for *hin*, a clear Burmese soup, so I ate that in the sitting room on a tray, at home with my parents. I swallowed it to placate the others inside of me. They wanted more, but I washed it down with a glass of lemonade and a Tunnock's Teacake.

All through my twenties, I ran to catch the train to London as if it were a sleigh to Lapland. Everything twinkled over there. My parents' home in Hillingdon, recently named in a poll by the *Daily Mail* as 'Britain's unhappiest town', was just a hole inside of a tree inside of a burning forest and I knew it was me that lit the flame. Someone had once thrown eggs at me from a moving car, the shell surprisingly sharp against my cheeks. They didn't do things like that in the world I was heading towards in the future. They only threw words around, like hard-edged discs which were avoided, again and again, with syntax, rhythm, punctuation. What I didn't know then was that passive aggression, the colonial par excellence, stung harder than the eggs, cut me for longer, cut me into squares of oblivion shaped like just them. At least I could stand over the sink and wash away the egg, but words burrow down, don't they? They form chapter headings in your book of life and no matter how much you try to change the story, you know that those titles are always going to encapsulate the main themes.

It sucks energy, always thinking about all these things. Sometimes, I have to concentrate on small things, making my world smaller so that I can go on. I distract myself with the red and silver foil from the Tunnock's Teacake wrapper. I study an image of a woman's hand in a painting. I spend hours writing about a particular shade of blue. I lose myself in the detail.

As the years went on, I added more of the black nail polish to my fingertips and I tried to read in French. Little sparrow with her mouth opening and opening, always ready to accept more knowledge. I completed my studies and began to teach undergraduate students in small seminar groups. Back then, there would be the requirement to teach just the one seminar group, not repeat teaching across a cohort which was nearing three figures, atomised into smaller parts.

I wrote countless academic papers, book chapters, and published my PhD. The fashionable, French feminist writings of Simone de Beauvoir, Hélène Cixous, Luce Irigaray and Julia Kristeva all played their part, but it was not simply academic ideas that I swallowed. There were endless lists of things only I held in my head – ways to pronounce words, ways to move my body, ways to hold my spoon and fork. How to pause, how to retreat. Frankenstein's little monster jerking around with my Sellotaped head and limbs, always ready to munch on the exquisite plates of colonialism and capitalism at the heart of the business of academia, full of juicy affectations, codes and rules I had to know or else be banished. All this became second nature. I became addicted to the feeling of passing for something else, anything except me. I practised the theory, body and soul.

I read the arts pages of the *Daily Telegraph* and compared them, studiously, with the ones in the *Guardian*. I learned how to order fine wine in restaurants and the subtle tonal differences between charcoal thread and black thread when it was woven into an artisanal sweater. I learned words like *moules marinière, faux pas, trompe l'oeil*. I never wore jeans and I didn't wear pearls because I knew that would be a step too far. The Queen wore pearls, or Madonna in her earlier years. The Chinese actress Anna May Wong wanted to be like Hollywood star Pearl White, but she had to make do with just the pearls themselves, which she was photographed in many times. Anna was always the self-sacrificing Madam Butterfly or the Dragon Lady – orientalist stereotypes she never truly escaped from because of how she looked. No, I would not wear pearls. Pearls of wisdom, those are the only pearls I covet.

Then, one day a 'caramel lowlights', toned Californian academic came to a conference in Cambridge in a grey Juicy Couture tracksuit, which, at the time, was often the choice of clothing favoured by Britney Spears. Britney has never been, and never will be, an academic's style icon. The girl wore very large hoop earrings and hot pink lip gloss. At some point between the filter coffee and moderately priced biscuits break and the sponsored wine reception, she presented a paper entitled 'The Early Modern French Aesthetics of Desire and Sex in Cyrano de Bergerac'. She was an enigma. My fascination with this girl overtook the entire conference. I studied her like a de Beauvoir biography. I walked slowly behind her, just to get a closer look at the earrings and the grey tracksuit – the most insistently obstinate of colours. Not even black... No one else gave her a second glance, but I did. She did not follow the rules. In fact, she didn't give a fuck about the rules and flaunted it with the kind of audacity that was so good it was hiding in plain sight, behind its own 'Americanness'.

Everyone else assumed she was simply being 'American', but I knew she had chosen the look because, you know, it was a distinctive look, to undermine the very rules of academia and the exact seat of power she was visiting. She was sticking two fingers up at this particular ivory tower. My conclusion: she was super confident. More than that: she was a G O D D E S S. She was golden, like her earrings and her Californian body. I could never have her body, so I made do with the black skirts and tights I wrapped my bones within, in mourning for a version of myself I could never possess.

I struggled on. Doubling up on my knowledge and the knowledge of that knowledge. Footnotes. Endnotes. Circles of academics that I watched from afar. Journals and peer reviews. Methodologies and paradigms. Polemics. Structural analysis, post-structural analysis, semiotics and linguistics. Freud and Lacan. I replaced my eyes with heavy stones which were altarpieces to a culture my own body did not recognise. My ancestors tutted and shook their old, wobbly heads, ashamed. I told them to lie still, accept the binding, because we all needed to walk in this life and, perversely, that always involved chains. I loved the beauty of the French feminists, their poetic symmetry of thought. They turned patriarchy inwards and created their own realm of semblance. I wore more layers of black nail polish and glided towards the inner circle of the High Priestesses. It was so beautiful there, touching the hem of their expensively understated garments.

I was one of 'them'. No one knew I came from one of the most 'deprived parts of London', where friends on free school meals asked me to steal basic bras for them in Marks and Spencer because I had an 'innocent face'. No one knew my mother's greatest ambition was to purchase a fake leather three-piece suite from Argos (my God, how she wanted that sofa). No one knew my parents had left me on my own to watch television, endlessly, throughout most school holidays, rarely interacting with me because World War II had robbed them of their own childhood and neither was able to grasp what a normal childhood looked like.

I won a place on a week-long retreat in Liverpool with Irigaray, along with a select group of other PhD candidates from all over the world. In her early seventies and often dressed in what appeared to be a quaint version of a sailor suit (striped T-shirt and navy jacket with fussy buttons), she enthusiastically drew diagrams in order to explain the thinking behind books such as *An Ethics of Sexual Difference* and *Speculum of the Other Woman*. There appeared to be many circles and Venn diagrams; at first this was charming, but then the frequency of these increased and we struggled to keep up. In the end, the circles became a sort of running joke – *there she goes again with the big 'O's*. After the immense pressure and fear associated with meeting one's idol, we were glad of time in the local pub, where we laughed so hard that our stomachs ached and our eyes watered. Such a relief, such a joy, to be together like that. Once we had all decided to step humbly out of the elite circle of academia and into reality, the whole week was a lot easier and much more fun.

Luce seemed to enjoy a walk after class. During one of these walks, I watched her stop for a moment near a playground. Her eyes were following the movements of two small girls clambering up a slide from the wrong end, fidgeting at its base. She told us how much she loved children's minds: *Their brains are like sponges at this age... Isn't that fascinating?* Childless, yet surrounded by her coterie of young female academics, she seemed as curious and as full of life as the two children she had seen playing. I wondered what knowledge we would pass on and if there was still time to learn, to remain 'spongy' in a world full of sharp edges.

In the realm of academia, I was in my own Brideshead, stepping into vaulted, ceilinged halls, eye to eye with depictions of Mary in the stained glass of college chapels, and eating dinners at candlelit tables, taking rides in balloons at summer balls. Social mobility, cultural mobility, was itself characterised by being mobile, flying, in fact. You can't see the details from up there, the small print, the terms and conditions. Assimilation is not a bitter pill; it has a sweet first tang, a fizz, which lines your stomach and warms your bones. In the world of academia, no one knew my mother could barely write, her handwriting not much better than my paternal grandmother's stroke-afflicted scrawls, and my father worked a part-time job in a hardware store, semi-retired after years of driving forklift trucks in a warehouse in Staines while whistling to the radio and smoking Old Holborn roll-ups on his tea break.

At a conference, a young female peer approaches me and tells me I look nice; I know her entire CV, she has been to Oxford and is dressed in a matching cornflower-blue two-piece from, I presume, Jigsaw. It's the wine reception, but I rarely enjoy drinking so I watch her with her half-empty glass and she totters over to me in kitten heels. She tells me I have a nice face and that I should use it more. At that moment, I felt my face slip off my shoulders and melt into the floor like the clock faces of the pocket watches in Salvador Dali's *The Persistence of Memory.*

Use my face for what, I immediately thought. Then it occurred to me that this Oxford girlie perceived my otherness as an advantage, but didn't get the fact that I was running away from it and I liked living in denial – that's why I was there at the bloody conference, holding a glass of orange juice and breathing in the specifically middle-class, educated and elite atmosphere like the sociopathic junkie from Hayes that I knew I was. She was holding out a pair of scissors and offering them to me like they were a gift: she was giving me career advice in the form of decapitation. *Snip, snip, snip.* Here we go again. After all this soul searching for an intellectual purpose, someone with actual intellectual credentials and a (cornflower) blue-blooded education to boot reminds me that I'll never leave my body behind and it's my fate to bear eternal witness to its ruins on the floor, again and again, as the 'scissors' are passed around. I wished she hadn't mentioned my face, because whenever we met again over the course of my entire career, I pictured her with the scissors and I wanted to run.

After my PhD, I rode a wild carpet ride through all of art history and women's creativity. I taught undergraduates and postgraduates about women filmmakers and artists, spinning their ideas around more ideas, metaphors, abstractions. Together, we looked at the meaning of things while I buried the meaning of me. I got a job at a lower-tier university, which was a miracle at any rate, given how unlikely it is for anyone to get work in academia. My students were gorgeously affable, kind, as clever as anyone at a more academic university, but often lacking confidence because they were, after all, at a former polytechnic, and they didn't quite believe in themselves because they often came from backgrounds that meant they didn't feel entitled. Each lecture felt like a little transformation. A small win. I wrote book after book, hymns to the clarity of my mind and 'freedom' to think. Escape. Hope. Civility.

In my thirtieth year, I moved to the semi-suburban fringes of England's green counties and I had a baby boy, which also meant I could only work part-time. I read books into the late hours and I wrote as soon as he was asleep. I kept going, I kept going, but I could not get a promotion, nor could I seem to get any more than a fractional contract, even when my baby was grown and at pre-school.

Feeling increasingly powerless, I did other jobs outside of my main job, like curation or art criticism. I tried to find a way to still be me, to have agency in a world that was slipping away from me. I got commissioned as a freelance arts journalist. Then I had another baby. Two boys and the world kept spinning. My world shrank and I sat in the near dark, watching the pictures change on my phone as I doomscrolled through early motherhood. My eyes filled with blue light from the devices that kept me company while babies slept in forty-five-minute cycles.

All the knowledge in the world could not stop my first baby from crying. He had my hieroglyph eyes. I was so tired that I fell asleep with him on the sofa. I dreamed I was in the head of a lion. Not just any lion, but a Burmese lion like the one I had seen on jars of pickled shrimp and chilli paste in my mother's house. I saw the lion consume me and instead of terror, I recalled Caravaggio's painting of a boy bitten by a lizard. My education seemed to interrupt the dream. But someone had corrected my reference points towards more erudite origins. This is when I began to remember Descartes, there, on the sofa, while my baby finally slept and I awoke, looking at the ceiling, or rather its splintering cracks where the old plaster-work was failing. Somewhere between those cracks, the ghost of Caravaggio. It wasn't the dream that had plucked Descartes from the withering ether of my mind, suffused then with dopamine from the all the breastfeeding and the thick fog of intellectual numbness, but what followed from that dream.

A pale brown, fat-bodied spider, as large as the rim of a sherry glass, had looped its way down from the ceiling on its spindly web and made its home on my left shoulder. I killed it with one hand before I had even thought about it. I had barely moved. My baby was still asleep on my chest. I wiped my wet, sticky palm on the side of the sofa, allowing a few fragments of the broken spider limbs to kiss the upholstery.

It was then that I started to understand something new about knowledge and the instinctiveness that comes from being in the world – this is all we will ever truly know. If something steals away our body, we will lose that connection forever. I had forgotten the earth and how I was born touching its sides, its completeness, its edges, connected breath by breath to the universe and the cosmos. Already, I had spent too long staring at screens. I had no idea of what was yet to come.

My school friend Malika once kissed her teeth at our English teacher in secondary school while the teacher was trying to explain the nuances of Coleridge. She hadn't meant to curse the teacher, but it was what her body wanted to do, so she did it. We were beyond it at that point. Our headmaster had famously walked off with all the funds and was wanted by the police. For the record, in my fifteenth year, the 1996 Ofsted report for the Hayes Manor School (Hillingdon, West London) is tonally woeful and apathetic:

> Whilst the standards of attainment are well below the national averages, they are commensurate with those in similar schools.

It's hard not to connect that damning line with another few lines which appear earlier:

> Forty-three per cent of the pupils are eligible for free school meals, well above both local and national

averages… About a fifth of the pupils are refugees, including asylum seekers; the predominant country of origin is Somalia. About a third of the pupils are white. More than half the pupils have English as an additional language (EAL) which is very high, and a significant proportion of them requires additional support to learn English. There are 35 different mother tongues represented in the school population, the main ones being Punjabi, Somali, Gujarati and Farsi… The ability range of the intake as indicated by the end of Key Stage 2 tests and cognitive ability tests shows a strong skew towards the lower ability end with few pupils of the highest ability represented.[2]

We were all predicted fails or very low grades at GCSE and beyond. Some of my peers were already retaking the first year of their BTEC specialist work-related qualifications (Business and Technology Education Council) or A levels, if they were lucky enough to be accepted on to the course. I was going to do OK, but we all knew we were destined to work nearby at Heathrow Airport or the local warehouses like our parents. Many of us were already working part-time at the airport, careers mapped out before we had even finished school.

Towards the end of our last year at school, my most eccentric friend, 'Vicomte de Valmont', as he liked to be called back then owing to his obsession with the film *Dangerous Liaisons*, encouraged me to go to an open day with him at the highly prestigious Slade School, University College London. We didn't know it at the time, but decadence awaited us: Bloomsbury squares and all of their hallowed architecture; blossom on the trees and blue plaques everywhere with names we'd never heard of. The feeling was beautiful, even though we understood it was on the other side of a piece of glass we would never be able to break or fracture with our fists. Beyond that glass was Graham Sutherland, Lucian Freud, Roger Fry, Dora Carrington, Ithell Colquhoun, Paula Rego, Stanley Spencer, Mona Hatoum and Rachel Whiteread. Others had brought their portfolios – we brought nothing but our attention and ill-informed curiosity. Our art teacher had taught us precisely nothing, simply prioritising more important things like smoking a fag or eating crisps round the corner in the room where the pottery kiln was housed. I'm surprised he didn't spontaneously combust or explode, just like all the other things that went near that kiln.

We listened to a talk about one of the Slade's most famous graduates, the post-impressionist British artist Gwen John. Despite being currently enrolled on an A level in Art and Design, we'd never heard of John so we just gazed up at the pictures from the projector. We lolled back in our seats and whispered to each other, complaining, albeit half-heartedly, of hunger or boredom. We had no point of reference for John's *Landscape at Tenby* (1896–1897) or *A Corner of the Artist's Room in Paris* (1907–1909). Deprived of the cultural means through which to understand any of the subject matter, I felt myself fall into the folds of the paintings and they settled and glimmered inside my body, making odd shapes and whispering in gentle harmonies, while the colonial voices inside me nodded and simultaneously criticised John's use of texture, her affected placement of a chair, her choice of medium (oils). I tried to touch the face of John's portrait of a little girl who stared lovingly at her mother as they walked along the shore at Tenby, fascinated by her gaze. Then, 'Vicomte' grabbed my hand and squeezed it, announcing he had had enough. We bid farewell to the other students (because we were raised to have manners) and then legged it to KFC for lunch.

My friend takes a photo of me with his imaginary camera: 'Girl in Bloomsbury, 1997'. Which was better, the KFC or Gwen John? One thing sated an immediate hunger, while the other gave me the taste of something new that would last a lifetime. A few years later, we both graduated, him in a black velvet suit and me with my hair down and two little 'horns' pinned up, in a bold homage to the hairdo made popular at the time by 'Scary Spice'.

The Fates spoke to me, as much as they spoke through Malika's lips. As a joke, I once predicted that a girl called Rajinder was going to marry at nineteen and have many children. I repeated this information to her face. It wasn't much of a prediction, but she was highly offended. We all knew it to be true, but to speak it aloud as an insult deeply disturbed her. While I had hoped to cheat my own fate, Rajinder would not be able to, and neither would most of my school friends. The laughter, the kissing of the teeth, was a rebuttal of the highest order, emboldened by what I don't know, fate, perhaps. Failing to produce her homework on Coleridge's 'The Nightingale', Malika simply shrugged and made an abject sound which, once and for all, told the Fates to fuck off.

I never forgot the laughter that followed before Malika was sent outside the classroom. She was still laughing in the corridor, blowing a crappy bubble with the Juicy Fruit gum she turned in her mouth. Perhaps she had simply meant to blow a bubble instead of making that slow tutting sound. A couple of years later she was thrown in jail overnight for defending her little brother in the playground, attacking a teacher in the blind fury of it all. Promising to be good, she enrolled herself at Ealing Tertiary College, admittedly a step up from Hayes Manor, and then trained as a nursery school teacher. I like to think of her laughing with a smirk on her face, because she always knew her own mind and I admired that. 'Knowing your own mind' isn't as easy as it sounds. Remember, you also have to know your own body. Malika knew who to fight for and she would never stop, body and mind.

I had broken the rules of space and time and someone had to pay. I should never have escaped my fate (or indeed, for that matter, the UK's 'unhappiest town'). My friend had kissed her teeth at the Fates, but it was me who had defied them most of all. They were seething. I was sitting in the imaginary halls of Brideshead as an academic, being paid good money to talk about art and revolution, beauty and desire. Even before I had sat in halls at King's College, Cambridge, about to give a paper in the French Department as a research student, I had somehow ended up at one of those notoriously posh summer balls at St John's College, Cambridge, thanks to a friend I had met while temping in Uxbridge (we're still friends). I had betrayed my ancestors and was wearing the sheep's clothing of a person I had invented and then become through sheer willpower.

Then, a plague arrived in my fortieth year and the laughter got louder and louder in my head. I found myself living in rural England, the furthest out of London I had ever been, where the slumping, weather-worn cows made their archaic, bassline bellowing in the cornfields outside my house while all of the world shut all of its doors. My Padaung ancestors returned the brass coils to their necks and tried to elevate themselves, higher up my body, near my vocal cords, but still they could not get out. A midwife once told me babies tend to turn towards their mother's heartbeat in utero if they sense she is distressed and now my ancestors were doing the same thing, their little heads turning, turning, trying to hear my bloodlines crackle and hiss, which were also their bloodlines crackling and hissing. They touched their necks and prayed. I couldn't hear them because their voices still sounded like they were at the bottom of a well.

Another prayed for me too. From the very lips of Saint Sidwella came a call to arms, a loving gesture. She tried to keep me in the living world where the fritillary butterflies landed on pink valerian, sow thistles, nettles; where the ragged foxes slid under yesterday's blooms deep, deeper still, beneath the newly shorn, blunted hedgerows, the widening shade of the cedars and the elms. Spring arrived and her stalking shadow came by, approaching me from the fields outside my house, her eyes wide discs of light that dazzled and shone, as silvery as the dew on the grass, flecked with their rolling, blinking moisture. She was holding her head in her hands – her voice emanating from the thin spaces between her fingers, which were illuminated with a pure and intense light. This, too, I could not accept because I was no longer there. I was under the spell of my computer screen's bewitching, myopic gaze.

I heard laughter again from behind the screen I was working on and then all of a sudden the world around me altered from black to blue, to blue to black, and back again. Or, more accurately, all was aglow beneath shifting shades of *blue light*. Soon, I would learn that the blue light was the colour of an explosion on a battlefield, as my ancestors and the Fates fought to the bitter end, thrashing and gripping each other by the neck, surrounded by an impenetrable ring of blue flames. Whatever it was, it was inside and it was outside. It pulled me in all directions. My body, a battleground. There was no time to talk, yet talking was all I did. The words pulsed and thrummed with their own persistent beat, burning bright blue and vermilion behind my eyes and ears. White noise, blue terror.

Saint Sidwella was still calling me out to the fields, but I didn't listen so she called upon the rain. The water flowed, the water rose. The floods came, as they always did in these parts of the country where I lived, but I was already under the waterline, inside the streams of data which were churning out of the technological hell hole I was in — and all that world was aflame. The water, which ran off the floodplains and the moors further north and south of my house, couldn't put the flames out, nor diminish the scripts of smoke that were rising from my own fingers. The smoke was my past, present and future on fire. Like Saint Sidwella, I found myself with my head in my hands and I was floating in the light of a thousand Zoom meetings. I watched all of my edges and ends being cut away. That bitterly persistent feeling of falling, or being folded, so that I would fit perfectly inside the stammering lines upon lines of those ever expanding, scrolling rivers in the sky.

Purgatory, for me at least, came in the shape of a single sash window overlooking wheat fields in Deep England. In the blue-black darkness, I thought about how I had become confused. Who was the tormentor and who was tormented? I was caught inside something. That something felt more than a bit like a Yayoi Kusama infinity pool of tragic irony, pathos and awkward silences. I turned off the screen and then I turned the screen back on again. I put my headphones in.

Is anyone there?

Is anyone there?

Can you hear me?

Can you all unmute yourselves and put your cameras on, if you can, please? We're about to start.

POSSESSIONS

I heard myself swallow hard and then I heard the delayed echo of that sound through my earphones. I bit my lip and then it was a few seconds later before that image of me biting my lip appeared on the screen, glitchy, shivering. Three bars of internet reception. Two bars. I turned off my camera. I peered out from above the blue light and listened carefully.

Just before we start, let's remind ourselves of the Danish folk tale 'Gold Heart'. There's a lovely girl entering a forest. She is so kind. She wants to be loved. She's wearing the most beautiful dress. All the animals ask her for things. Every one of them. She keeps giving everything away until she has nothing (we won't talk about why the animals are like this at the moment, for the purpose of the story). She takes off her dress. She offers that, too. She is so trusting. She is being so 'good'. Suddenly, she is struck by lightning and dies. Wham. The whole of the forest took every part of the girl for themselves. They sheltered under her dress, they coveted her possessions and in doing so, possessed her. By the time she was struck by lightning, she was already gone and death was merely a kindness. One final erasure for good measure.

Now, my friend kisses her teeth. She points and she tells

me I'm not really the good girl naked in the forest. *Look,* she says, laughing somewhere behind my head.

Look at you, you're the fucking lightning.

Is anybody there?

As the light of the computer screen entered my vision and tried to zap me with its penetrating laser flares, I felt something at the sides of my body. It was attaching itself to me, weaving itself into my skin. It tasted of the bitter roots of the banyan trees in Burma and the windswept heather on Dunkery Beacon in England. It was the colour of gently swaying poppy fields in the Burmese Shan States, bristling with an incandescence which rolled into ancient vistas I had once known and loved at various points in my life.

This feeling drew itself up into the shape of deep, deep shadows that passed silently over mountainsides in Ireland, Scotland and Wales. I recalled the scissor-shaped arches of cathedrals I had visited, the uneven steps within a priory in Exeter. As if they were staves of music dancing across a page, I saw configurations of crows chasing over the notched contours of the Devonshire valleys near my home; my children's hands tracing the lids of ice on puddles where there was once a hornet's nest within the hollow trunk of a fallen yew tree. A sparrow flying out of a glass porch.

I knew these things before I had understood anything else.

I was heading back to earth, to something elemental and true. Motherland, mother soil, whatever it was, I was now clutching it. It rose up from my skin and it formed words in the sky.

These are the words.

2
Floppy Cats

Some Important Terms:[3]

Blended learning

Blended learning, also known as hybrid learning, is an approach to education that combines online educational materials and opportunities for interaction online with traditional place-based classroom methods.

Asynchronous learning

When used in an educational context, asynchronous learning refers to courses where students access course materials – lectures, readings and assignments – in their own time. Learning, in other words, takes place at all different times for students enrolled on a course, because there's no set class time.

Synchronous learning
Synchronous learning refers to instructors and students gathering at the same time and place (virtual or physical), thus interacting in 'real time'.

I had been coughing for a few months, following a trip to London to talk about some rococo art in a gallery near Mayfair. I coughed before the plague came.

I dissolved vitamin C tablets into little cups of water. I added an extra sprinkling of echinacea as if it were a special healing potion, but the reality of it was that I knew the cough would worsen anyway.

In the lane between our houses, a Lycra-clad neighbour was keen to tell me she had seen the news from London (proximity is everything) and called it 'propaganda'. *I shouldn't worry*, she said, mid-sprint in the panting half-shade of her two large Labradors. I opened my mouth to speak and then I simply inhaled the air that sat between us. My neighbour did not wait for a reply. I found myself unable to move so I simply stood there for a while under the blossoming boughs of the ash trees, their foliage seeming to stretch and yawn over our heads. I felt my left hand rummaging around in the pockets of my jacket, my fingers searching for my keys, my phone, my sanity.

I lay down and my heart beat rapidly, my body became covered in sweat and I was thirsty all the time, as if I had spent the night at some kind of techno house party from the late 1980s. My muscles ached, too, perhaps because I had been dancing all night at that party and I had forgotten to sit down. But of course there were no more parties anymore. There was no one to dance with except my sons in our kitchen in a house which faced wheat fields in England.

All we had to do was stay inside. My chest was raw and I wanted to sleep, but I couldn't because my eight-year-old and four-year-old were downstairs and there was homework to be done. My partner did the maths while I coughed through several PhD examinations (online), more lectures (online) and more A-level classes, which I did to cover the extra bills because academia on a part-time basis doesn't pay very well.

I sorely missed the small ceremony of tea and individually wrapped biscuits that would usually accompany a two-hour PhD *viva voce*. Meanwhile, I planned an academic conference that was going to be held in person and spent a vast number of hours calculating the catering bill. I had to request orders via the labyrinthine world of College Services and Hospitality (£2.00 per cup of tea/coffee). There was also smoked salmon, guinea fowl and Cornish lamb. Sadly, we could only afford the 'light bites' menu, which mainly consisted of houmous.

I took on more work at a few other universities, including one that was posher than the one I was permanently, albeit fractionally, employed at. I liked the sound of the posh university. Though I had never physically been there, I started to work at this other university online. Really, I could have been anywhere, but the vibe was definitely not anywhere, it was distinct, specific, meticulous in its machinations and the opacity of its power structures. This place had money, power, status and it was very keen to retain it all. This university did very well during the 2021/2022 tax period, achieving gross profits that tipped towards a billion pounds. (To put this into perspective, Tesco made almost six billion, but a billion is a still a lot, right?)

This particular university I had joined was not the winsome, shaggy dog of a polytechnic (with smart buildings) I had known for over a decade. It was living royalty, a sovereign state whose logo, I imagined, could easily be a single red tower from a medieval castle with a crown, at a jaunty angle, tumbling from its highest point. In another life, the logo might have been part of a sleek, new tarot card set, because it very much resembled 'The Tower', the sixteenth card in the Major Arcana, which always represented crisis, materialistic thought, destruction and 'Higher Education'. Glancing at the university's website and intranet pages, I wondered again why

I was still 'doing' academia. There had been reports of lecturers at other universities sleeping rough in tents because they couldn't afford accommodation. Redundancies. There were countless strikes and disputes. I was precariously employed, temping, a status even lower than the lowly lecturer or tutor, hourly paid and vulnerable, but I had to work so I turned on my screen and grabbed my earphones. I tried not to think about the things I knew: I knew there were many others, mostly males, being paid double my salary for doing the same thing; I knew I was one of only two working mothers in the entire staff room; I knew my face and my mind didn't fit. For a moment, I tried to jam my face and my mind into the squares they had made for themselves on the grid within the system.

The male lecturers brought their cats to the departmental Zooms, cradling them, while my very un-catlike son struggled with his maths homework downstairs. He let out a scream each time we mentioned fractions. The men and their cat-babies greeted each other with the kind of dialogue you would only hear in a gentleman's dining club, their floppy hairstyles matching their floppy cats. Hushed 'hellooos' bounded round. 'Good morning' (there's nothing good about it). After about ten robotic, perfunctory minutes of this they would acknowledge me and then go back to stroking the cats. So many cats. Perhaps the cats were our clandestine leaders, only we didn't know it yet. They purred so softly into my headphones. The French filmmaker Chris Marker believed cats were never on the side of power. He used an image of a cat instead of a signature. Maybe Marker wasn't right about all the cats, after all.

At one of the departmental meetings, I'm watching the Zoom, but I'm not there. I've turned my camera off. In the lower left corner of the screen, something shuffles along with human features. I see the meek wife of one of the professors serve her husband tea on a tray while he talks. She was still in her pyjamas. She backed out of the shot and he sipped the tea, continuing as if she wasn't there at all. I wondered if this was for her benefit or for his. It seemed to me that to admit his wife's existence would unsettle the carefully curated air of blank, clinical professionalism that he exuded at all times. The experience of the pandemic taught me that academics, at their worst, are like any other tribe of corporate cronies, but probably worse still, because their elevated roles as superior intellectuals, with titles to prove it, left barely any room for humanity to thrive. They believed themselves to be higher beings. Kindness seemed to flee from their cold hearts while my own feelings seemed to enlarge. I felt everything and I could not stop. We see inside the homes of people who preferred to be unshackled to any semblance of life outside of the institution. What matters most is that the Zoom makes the cerebral, civilised academic ever more civilised and literally detached, even from their own homes: a dream come true. A talking head on screen, forever exerting control and authority. Their bodies are absent, but the unnamed wives are still crawling on the John Lewis carpeted floor.

Was academia always like this or was I the one who'd changed? It doesn't matter. The only thing I knew to be true was that I was looking at something monstrous. Over on the screen, the talk of business continues, digital content appearing just like the emperor's new clothes. But what if the body underneath those clothes has changed? The body is now a great, rippling, over-sized beast with seven heads and toes shaped like hooks. So, we are in that moment now, the moment where the beast is trying out the new clothes and everyone applauds, but instead of a naked emperor, this whole new clothes business has revealed the fact that we are all dealing with a manifestly power-wielding, mutated beast.

I think there were a lot of male academics receiving cups of tea from non-present wives during the pandemic, their tea-drinking upholding the imperialist values of their institutions while their families became little wild colonies of abandon: cereal-coated carpets, broken TV sets, taps left running, bins tipping over. Empty gin bottles lolling against each other in the recycling bin (we know for sure that gin sales went right up around about this time). There is a statistic somewhere proving male academics were the most productive during the pandemic, while female academics carried the burden of home-schooling and other domestic activities in addition to their workload and thus produced rather a lot less. Production = promotion and more pay. The truth no one dares speak is that no one should be teaching at all, that is, if we were to be totally honest about this. We should all be running for the hills, because none of this is urgent, but yet it is, *it is*, because money has exchanged hands and there are now thousands of students logging on to the portals, the Zooms, the library pages.

Six months on from the first lockdown and the system continues to operate online as well as 'face to face', so the corporation have much to gain in spite of their pandemic 'losses'. I have slid through some kind of thinning portal in which I am being paid to talk into a screen, mostly listening to the sound of my own voice interspersed with silence, while chaos occurs outside of the screen and is being made more chaotic, deliberately, for the sake of ~~EFFICIENCY~~ profit.

As for the ones with the virus, they are testing them IN THE SAME BUILDING as the one being used to teach in, 'blended', of course. The professors have a look of terror on their faces, which morphs into stoicism and then blankness. It's the blankness I hate the most. No one talks about the coughing and if someone does cough, they say 'excuse me', and then carry on as if trying to swallow down their humanity. In spite of all this, I do actually want to scream and hug them all at the same time, violently shake them out of their blankness, but my body is still speaking, still on the call.

I frantically try to locate my students on the Zoom, in the room, in the breakout rooms, on the register, on social media (hey, that works). Some have left the breakout rooms. I count them. Numbers scroll like digital data from *The Matrix*, falling in rows upon rows of streams, coding itself, again and again into an everlasting algorithm of CONSUMER/SUPPLIER binaries. I was caught in the supply chain, but I refused to deliver the 'product' the way it should be delivered: dead-eyed, detached and fact-laden. My fingers hover over the keyboard as I try to work out what the moral ground is here, what the feeling, the *sense* is, to any of this. I've been stranded in an abbey and I'm waiting for a messiah, but there's only 'Siri' or 'Alexa'. I glare at the single sash window in the bedroom where I teach, staring out at the lambs in the fields. These lambs, I think, they are as bound to their fate as I am now.

I try to generate the code for the register, but no one has told me how to use any of the systems, so I'm guessing all the time. I don't speak sentences anymore, I simply shout into the air, *Where are my earphones, where are my earphones! It's not logging on, it won't connect!* The register proves the 'present-ness' of everyone, though it's just more data because, as we all know, you can be present while someone is talking but you can be elsewhere in your head, or you can log on and turn off the microphone, the video, and still be present. 'Presentness' is a mental state, never a code. Never a QR code, never a barcode, never a number. Still, I feel strangely calm. I'm too old for this to intimidate me. I'm running with it. I think of my childhood friends now with full-time jobs at Heathrow Airport. I think of the nurses and the carers in the hospitals and care homes.

I close my eyes and listen to the sheep outside. Thankfully my camera is off. I'm a disembodied voice, an enchantress. I am all voice and no body. I step out of my body and into the Matrix. My blood evaporates into nothingness. Invisibly, I scale the perimeter of all the things, weightless, while sylla-bles and vowels swoop and slide. In the bleak, blank ether of these infernal streams, perhaps I've come here to hide.

How long before I stop being able to choose which entity I dwell within?

Who is in my body if I'm *out there* in the data stream? Like stowaways on a ship, my Burmese ancestors are looking out from my eyes while they take care of my body. They are lighting fires and waiting for the moon to shine. They are exhaling their breath into me and I am breathing. I am breathing and I am speaking, but I'm not there. I've passed my body over to the data stream and all the young people are waiting to accept me. I hope they pass everything back. I hope. My only real wish is to return via the data stream to my family while I'm held in this condition of absence, levitating indefinitely between worlds. It's so dark in there, in the stream. Nothing lives for long out there in the darkness. Even astronauts have contact with mission control so that they might find their way home. Every night I send myself out into the stars.

I hold on to the thought of my youngest son waiting for me to read him a story at the edge of the world, in his bedroom overlooking wheat fields in England.

What if it wasn't me who came back? What if something took me away?

Minutes before I was about to start a guest mentoring session with a group of pioneering and Successful Women Artists,[4] I had been taking care of my youngest child and

I had burned some pasta in a pan, allowing the water to completely evaporate while I was caught up in some other chore elsewhere. Smoke. The fire alarm went off and all I could think of was getting some air into the kitchen, so I opened a large sash window and it pivoted the wrong way, falling on my head as if it were a trapdoor coming loose. Descending chaos. The window was on a special hinge that was supposed to make it easier to clean, sliding all the way up or down, but it was old and broken, so it had fallen forward as I struggled to let the air in. For a moment, I imagined a crack across my skull, wet where my fingers were about to part sections of my hair, searching for a fracture. A radiating pulse below my fingers. I tried not to fall over and sat on the floor with my apron on, a numbness moving across the back of my head and then over my shoulder blades. Pressure from the air above. To my relief, there was no blood, but nevertheless I sat dazed, reliving the feeling of the weight of the glass and the force of the frame coming down on me. I knew then that I would have a headache for weeks afterwards.

I wondered how many other 'trapdoors' might fall on me and what shape they would take over the years. I imagined my bloody-minded, less-than-grown-up hieroglyph-self continued to run amok in the adult world, fleeing things that fell from the sky.

Later, in the Zoom, one of the artists tells me I needed to be 'in my body' and my clumsy error with the sash window might have been the result of too much thinking and not enough physical awareness. I needed to bring my mind back into my body. She was very wise. My thoughts needed to be anchored in my body. My body must be mission control. I have to hold on to myself holding on to myself – me holding on to me, an unending ladder of self-care. I can do this. I need to jump out of the way of falling windows and guide others, too, like a beacon in this bleak, bastard midnight in the history of modern civilisation. No pressure. Follow the blue light.

After several lectures, which are effectively me speaking for three to four hours without a great deal of interaction, I have a tutorial with an undergraduate called, well, let's call him Timothée Chalamet. He tells me he is at his parent's home in Belgium. He has called from, specifically, the kitchen island, to speak about his end-of-term essay (worth 60 per cent) on French cinema. Academia is 90 per cent confidence and 10 per cent citations, so I continue with grace and enthusiasm, encouraging him, nodding (there's always more nodding). His younger sister enters the kitchen and makes a strawberry and banana smoothie. *Chop-chop-chop, smash-smash, WHIZZzzzzz.* We stop talking to listen to the blender. She takes her time slapping the contents of the blender into a tumbler. I see the back of her head and her sweatshirt, which has a crest of arms on it, a French private school logo. She rests a casual, loving hand on T.C.'s shoulder, just for a second. He holds her hand there, smiling at her. *Laisse-moi tranquille!* She laughs and then I see her body exit the screen. I hear a small terrier yelp after her, its groomed tail flicking from side to side in the background. *That's my little sister. She's preparing for her school exams.*

Quietly, T.C. tells me he's afraid he won't finish his studies. He tries to tell me this in such a polite and apologetic way that I almost cry. *It doesn't matter, none of it matters right now. Go, go, hug your parents. Eat. Dance with your sister in the kitchen.* But I don't say any of that out loud, because I'm contractually obliged to do other things. At this point, there are procedures I have to recall. Each university has their own policy regarding student well-being, my well-being, the university and its 'well-being', so I continue hesitantly and suggest he gets in touch with student welfare. There are so many websites and email addresses. I hand these out like damp apologies.

Just behind his head, there is a painting of a French pastoral scene – a horse crossing a field with haystacks dotted across the landscape. The walls are an expensive cream, probably something like Farrow & Ball 'Dorset Cream' or 'Montagu Matt'. T.C. adjusts his Calvin Klein glasses and I see his very young, very lovely face. He looks like he is trying to be brave in a desperate situation. It's a look we've all perfected, but I know it's paper thin. He is so frightened and I want to help him, but we are not supposed to love anyone in these roles as lecturers/soothsayers/oracles. I feel everything and say nothing. I know I've the patience of a nurse and it's a skill largely wasted here, so I take the opportunity to lean into it because I don't know how else to do this. I smile back at him. I think very carefully about the exact tone of my voice. At the same time, I'm thinking about ideas I can share with him, books I think he will enjoy. I see myself smile back at him on the screen. Eventually, I present T.C. with several reading suggestions and an offer to meet again soon. He nods. I nod. I don't want to go. He doesn't want to go. If we were in an office, he would linger by the door. His hand would grip the door handle. He would fiddle with his folder or phone. It's the little things, isn't it? Human things. You can't do that here. It's very brutal. I give him my time, though the rules suggest fifteen minutes. I have only my time to give him. But you cannot care at this point. If you do, you're a goner. Caring for people is not productive and has no financial value in this transactional world. Where does all the caring go if it doesn't fit into this equation? If it's not professional, or a private obligation, but something else?

It starts as soon as I try to turn off the call. It won't log off. I cough again and I glimpse the smallest glint of green out of the corner of my eye, on my shoulder. Green, like sage and ochre-coloured lichen from Dartmoor, the rocks up at Haytor. My shoulder clicks and stiffens a little. I feel nauseous, a pain high up in my chest, but also low down in my stomach. There is a weird, unsettled feeling, as if someone is pulling on the corner of a bedsheet, exposing my cold, naked legs. Was it something I ate? I've not eaten yet. That's probably it. I shake it off. I wave at the screen and then – *blip* – T.C. has gone. I never see him again (he leaves the university). I still think of him now, years later. The boy with the soft brown curls who wanted to write about the French New Wave, while the world shimmied into all sorts of shades of mismatched colours and blurry textures; the wagging tail of a small terrier; the back of his sister's head. I try to imagine her face.

My shoulder and my head began to feel odd again. There were the tiniest of spikes behind my ears, as if something was drawing blood. I presumed it must have been the plastic eroding on the earphones. I threw them on the floor and coughed again. My throat was itching and burning, cat's claws down my neck, and then I just lay on the floor, my hands over my mouth. I could still feel the left side of my face twitching (the internet says this is due to stress and could lead to a stroke). I lie very still, but the left side of my face is fluttering, ticking, it refuses to be inanimate: a tiny butterfly in the space to the left of my chin and my lower lip. The butterfly beats its furious wings. *Tick. Tick. Tick.*

A conduit of emotion rather than a vacuum, a natural empath, I failed to shut myself off from the noise. My lectures *could* have been mere tarot readings. Trance-like. I *could* have spoken words I had spoken before, for many years, and just shuffled my PowerPoint slides with affected, meaningful pauses and changes in tone. But I decided to do more. The moment required much more. I cleared my mind of the shopping list I had to get through later, my son's English homework, the filthy cups piling up in the stainless steel sink, the heating bills, the electricity bills, the neighbour who died suddenly and my love for her. I cleared my mind so that I could fill *theirs*.

Every day I place my hands on the deck of the computer keys. Eyes looking ahead. *What will it be, then? What will speak out and what will retreat into the shadows?* I can hear grazing sheep outside. A lamb calling out. I see rising fog beyond the hedgerows, a scraggy lamb darting along the twisted border of the overgrown thicket, seeking out the warmth of its mother's fleece. Lambing season out there, while I shepherd my voiceless flock. One by one. One by one. *Hello there, welcome, Josh, Zoe, Sabine, Aliyah, Benji, Naz...* Lists, names without faces, I call them into being. It is an enchantment in a virtual room that keeps folding itself inwards, collapsing into smaller and smaller dimensions. I fold an origami shape from the air and my own breath, the bitter wind in the ash trees outside and the electrical systems which connect us all through the interface. Look, *an origami swan!*

I watched the blank, sparse sky hang like a sheet of tracing paper over whiteness, the clouds arranging themselves into a double-folded opacity while everything tipped sideways. I wished for that mute doubling of whiteness to enter my chest, to let it enter into my body. That tracing paper held over the sky – it's true, I desired it, that thought of erasure, oblique angles, numbness from everything around me. I wanted to be like the hollow, negative space in between the spruces that lined the ancient hills I could see beyond the fields; I wanted, no longer, any brightness of feeling, just the indifference of the gaps in between each branch of creation and what was to pass all around me, body and soul. Then, the memory came to me of the birth of my first son and the miracle of the immaculately well-timed epidural.

The jabbing of joints, the novelty of legs and feet becoming objects to pick at or to stab with the end of a mobile phone. The sensation of pins and needles when the drugs no longer cast their spell.

I blinked. I blinked again and then I felt myself screaming into every fucking fold of that origami swan. It was like trying to stop the very movement of the stars. All tumbled and turned as my body pinballed about the air and I tried to locate my own voice while it spun and clicked and scissored through a vortex of dead time and dead space. I concentrated on the shape of the swan and how its wings might herald a state of oblivion. No one was watching but, for the record, it would have been bloody obvious that I was on my knees. My knees were bent and my feet were tucked under my legs as I sat on the bed, hunched over. I could not feel a thing, nor could I move, because the blue screen that flashed before my eyes had placed a curse upon me and made a giant origami swan of whatever I was, whatever I had been before.

On my computer keyboard, I saw white feathers fall like lightning.

The sound of two New Holland tractors loading up deep layers of soil outside, levers being pulled, the bucket

lowering and plunging itself into the land. Seagulls pickpocketing the rubble. Their beaks like pale daggers. The distant yet immediately recognisable procession of someone on horseback moving through the lanes beyond the top field; their head and shoulders discreetly bobbing up and down, moving at a pace that is exactly horse-shaped and horse-hearted. They reach the end of the lane and then they disappear from view.

Tiny iron filings tessellate under my skin. Each thought and feeling afire, a comet, the wick of a candle lit before a storm.

I imagine myself transported outside. I jump out of my body the way a cat leaps back from a noise in the dark. I make a dozen haybales and stack them high. I arrange them like standing stones in a field. I watch the golden straw fly like embers.

Time speeds up. Hours pass like seconds. Day has turned to night and I watch its rotating projections. Pegasus makes a relic of my fears.

I am the horse's breath, the rounded heat of its hooves, the narrow corridor of flight where the seagulls soar, where the red, red dust comes loose from the old bricks of the barns and enters a spinning wind.

I talk for two hours because the students are not talking, mostly. Someone mistakenly turns on their microphone and I hear a police siren, chaotic noise from a crowded café, tyres of all shapes screeching along asphalt, car horns and engines revving. Laughter somewhere. Then the sound cuts off and I hear nothing again, except it is never nothing. My dog is drinking water downstairs, his tongue licking his ceramic bowl; the radiators yawn; blue tits fly up to the eaves of the house and their wings tap the glass as some small morsel of nesting material is picked from the slate tiles. Slowly, the Zoom is filled with minds trying to imagine clever things, while others simply try to imagine. We fill the time.

Imagination is a currency. No, better to call it a current or, here right now, a soundwave.

Hold on to that.

It's already in you, it is living in between and inside everything.

I keep a glass of water by the table. My gaze alternates between the image of my reflection in the glass and that of the one on my computer screen – two slippery versions of me trapped in a container. My students are listening and respond in the chat option running alongside the centre of the screen. Other than this, there is darkness. Other than this, the university is recording my every sound and movement before it's uploaded to the data 'cloud'. Each time I end a lecture, I receive a little link that automatically tells me the work is now ready to be added to my online materials. PING. I gather up so many of these links like multiple strands of DNA. After all, *I am* being uploaded. Parts of myself stored on the system start to resemble… not me, but me as info snacks which the system consumes day and night.

My *thinking* is stored on the system, but only the parts that matter to the institution, minus the actual process of thinking. The system obliviates the breath between the things that led to each thought as I went about my daily life, the sensations that collected up inside of my body and led to a thought, thoughts. That darting light fired up by mirror neurons and electrical impulses, shards of cognition and muscle memory learned over time. *Snip, snip, snip*: the memories of my mother walking me to school in the rain, the shape of a giant pillow I held under the arch of my back when I was pregnant with my first child, the taste of an orange Calippo. These things passed down through milk and blood, passed again through the cosmos and returned to me through a constellation of stars. *Topos. Logos*, as the Greeks would have it. Where, now, are those stars?

Every day, I am teaching, working, trying to explain and inspire, with so much passion and enthusiasm I could burst (to fabricate and manufacture this at the level required here is a problem I know I will have to face sooner or later). In other spaces of the digital multiverse, many of my colleagues are phoning it in, repeating all the old tracks they've used for years, but I'm going for it. They are droning on, half-interested, half-hearted. I am wide-eyed, wide-bodied, taking them all in and housing them within my entire self like a twinkling cathedral in some rural city. I make stained-glass windows for them in the shape of, tenderness and courage. I try, I try. I cut the glass, I cut the glass. For a moment, the colours make a lovely light. But I know, really, I'm cutting myself.

How long can this last? I'm running out of glass.

How could I *not* adjust, retune. I am stupidly optimistic, generous. I am taking books off the shelves at home and reading aloud from them. I am sending link after link after link to work I think will help, videos I have found, essays I have loved. *Look! Look at this!* For just one second, if I can help them feel the way I've felt about knowledge and how it can give you hope, then, I can mend something here. It's like I've got the thread in the eye of the needle and now I'm holding it between my fingertips. I can repair these holes in time, pass the thread through the patchwork strata of the old and new worlds of academia, stitch it all together and make something whole again. But while I'm holding that darning needle, all the time, all of that time, the university is recording me and that makes me nervous. I'll drop the needle, you see. They will simply carry on processing the raw data, processing the number of students attending and the sound of me speaking. The system is hungry for that data and that is what I'm being paid for – my energy, my passion, is superfluous, added value. The system can't see the holes, but I can. I'm sat here staring at all of these pathetically gaping, unravelling threads.

Beneath my feet, piles and piles of needles, all the needles I've ever dropped, all the hopes I've ever let slip through my fingers.

Wait, what's this…? I've been asked to co-teach with someone who has foolishly decided to put Union Jacks all over their PowerPoint slides in an effort to talk more generally about 'culture' without any specific intention or formal case study. I sense we've gone off-piste here; I sense the lecturer is also muddling on and, to be honest, I'm finding the optics a little jarring. Someone with no subtlety or life experience is performing politics in a volatile situation. I open my mouth to speak and then I close it again. No one asks me about these lectures. The management team are more concerned about the 'efficiency' of all the administration. I doubt anyone has checked the optics.

In addition to this, time signatures appear on most things so you can track when someone has opened a file on the SharePoint and the length of time they've spent looking at it. There are suggested reading times listed below each file to ensure my productivity is optimised. These times are based on average reading speeds, but this doesn't ever take into account diverse ways of learning or the fact that some of us are multilingual, so reading may 'look' and 'feel' different. I look at the little statement of time, which exists in a separate column next to the file, its truth taunting me because it is not my truth at all. Over on the workspace, it is clear that:

Reading = time

Marking =time

Meetings =time

(Looking at multiple Union Jacks on my screen without much context = time).

If you watch closely, most academics can attune themselves to a speed that perfectly matches the requisite length of conference papers or tutorials with students. Without ever looking at a clock, they are able to perfect the art of *knowing when to stop* and shutting down meetings after precisely fifteen to thirty minutes. Learned behaviour. During a meeting, you can tell when the conversation starts to slow down and there is more punctuation, more silence, before everything grinds to a halt and diaries are opened in order to schedule the next meeting. I know it's not just academics who do this 'timing' thing, but they do it with *excellence*. At presentations, the average conference paper is around fifteen minutes long and that equates to around about 2,000 words if spoken at a regulated speed (double-spaced), with pauses for emphasis. I failed miserably at this during my younger years as an *early career researcher*, going over by an embarrassing five or ten minutes, overhearing fellow panellists' boasting about how they had 'nailed it' while I stammered along with the microphones and bottles of spring water on side tables.

My mother knew the exact time it would take to boil just enough basmati rice in a pan for three people with only three cups of water. She would measure the rice out in the same Chinese-style teacup every day, tapping it against the pan as she turned up the heat. My aunt knew how long it would take to walk down the hallway of her Victorian house before she slid open the heavy, frosted glass door to the porch, where I would stand and wait for her on the doorstep. My father knew how long it would take to peel a mango. All of these measurements of time have no rooted- ness in language, no system to confirm their existence, to ensure they leave their mark. Rhythms, gestures, only I know or understand. This particular feeling for time cannot exist without love.

The earliest generation of farmers who had once worked the land out there, beyond my bedroom window, might have followed the phases of the moon in order to plan when to harvest their crops. Of course, agricultural methods were once derived from the rhythms of lunar activity. Cosmological time. What could I harvest now in the ruins of colonial time, the clock ticking inside of me, the one I heard inside my mother's belly, lodged in the place where her innocent heart should have been, while her blood and her mother's blood coursed through my veins, pulsing with languages I would never speak, places I would be born to love yet never truly experience for myself. I've inherited this colonial time: a mesh of absences, neither here nor there. Stillborn hours, days, years, stolen away by thieves in the night, long before there was even anything to take. Colonial time, like a game of pass-the-parcel and finding out there's nothing there at the end, cheated by all of those tightly wrapped layers.

As I evolved as an academic and found employment in Higher Education, my body adjusted to a new kind of time where words fitted more pleasingly into slots of temporality. Pauses existed only ever for dramatic effect. My voice spoke in crystalline patterns of near-perfect, oratory excellence. Even the pace of my walking was different (more graceful, I thought, slower and with better deportment). But I didn't just change my appearance, I corralled myself into thinking that time was also another form of imperialism. The chimes of that clock broke my bones and then reset them again each time I returned home from an academic conference, reading my well-researched and eloquently phrased papers with rehearsed perfection. I was hungry for that approval more than any other soul in the room. Or, let's just say that the others felt more entitled to it than I did. Between entitlement and indifference, I wanted the prize that told me I had been a good citizen, a perfect example of assimilation.

Over a decade later, I find myself inhabiting a moment in which there are no rooms, only Zooms. My colleagues can track my activity through the data and monitor my existence through this means of surveillance, which is freely available for all to access. Over on the other interface, in my Microsoft 365 Outlook mailbox and the SharePoint, NO ONE writes normal sentences. Everything is full of jargon and passive-aggressive pleasantries preceding casual, subtle criticism of marking, of performance. The system is monitoring everything, but for whose benefit? The dead-not-dead do micro-aggressions really well, but sometimes this violence is just simply a blunt force and it breaks through the surface of things.

A senior member of staff shouts at me on a Zoom and tells me to let them finish talking. I was trying to tell them something important. I can't remember what it was, but it *was* important. Everything is important. To be shouted at in your own home from a screen is something new to me. The coughing, the uncertainty, the crisis, that's now very familiar, but the insult is entirely new. The zombie bites my head off. It's hard to bear witness to that. Also, bearing witness requires some objectivity, distance. You have to jump out of your body to understand the wider implications of the thing that is happening before your very eyes. What if you are held in the space of victimhood? What, then? Can you still be a witness if you never told anyone about the things you saw? All this exists in an unreal space, in addition to all of the other unrealities, which keep spiralling into chaos.

They try to vanish me because they know I'll be going soon, anyway. To them, I'm just the magician's assistant and right now I'm being put into a box. They shift the box sideways and my head appears to become detached from my body, sliding to the left. Then, to the right. They close the doors to the boxes and they cover my face. It's a kind of slicing, but I feel no pain, not yet anyway. I'm still smiling under the spotlights, covered in sequins, blue glitter on my eyelids. My hand, somewhere impossible, high over my head, waving with my fingers. The whole thing spins and then I'm not in the box anymore. Ta-da! But it's hardly the greatest show on earth. They've made a vagabond of me, only fit for this circus.

I'm too old for this. I'm middle-aged and an 'esteemed' academic with a better research record and publications profile than most of my peers in this particular institution, but that doesn't stop one of them from asking me to let them finish speaking, raising their voice with irritation. I see them weigh up the imbalance of me. Of course, they decide I must be controlled. Muted. Made smaller. They ignore me at meetings. They tell me I'll never get a permanent job, because I need to get a research grant of at least half a million pounds. Is this a game? I have to win money in order to win a job, but the job will pay significantly less than the money I've won because of the overheads involved in processing and administrating that income. When I give a lecture, they suddenly pat me on the back like a college student on work experience. Fixed-term, precarious contracts mean that I'm only a hologram of a real person projected into a space where I function in timed intervals, speaking in incessant streams, yet can never be truly heard. I hear myself laugh. Some of them keep their heads down; they're sweet and when we meet in person, they try to reassure me and tell me things will get better. In the Zoom, I hear someone else laugh. A shadow at the edge of the screen.

She was there all along, my old school friend Malika, standing in the corner of the room, kissing her teeth, waiting to be asked to leave. She knows this is all absurd, so she just sits there in the corner, watching me with her eyes narrowing.

The screen goes dark again. It's also dark outside now, pitch black, and I find it hard to settle. My hands have become heavy and stiff. I notice that the skin around my knuckles has developed a rash that resembles green moss, spores, like stuff I've seen growing on the yew trees near where I live. I google it and assume it's a repetitive strain injury combined with an allergy to washing-up liquid (our dishwasher has broken). My thumbs won't flex towards the space bar on the keyboard. For a while, I type out everything without any spaces between the words. It feels like I am holding my breath, like someone else is doing the typing. I push the computer aside and scratch my hands again. When I look down, I realise I've scratched myself raw. Blood rising in little spots. Lichen-coloured clouds above my knuckles.

Outside, a lamb calls out again. A tiny bleating. A tractor pulls over in the field, flooding it with white light. The engine rumbles and then cuts out. A figure in the field, moving closer towards the lamb, precise and definite movements.

I hover my hands over the 'shut down' option on my computer. I click on it and watch all the windows on my screen disappear and all the systems logging out, one at a time. *Are you sure you want to log out?* Someone hasn't logged off the Zoom and I unmute myself one last time.

Hello… hello, are you OK? The lecture has ended now…
Hello?
Hello?
Nothing happens. Then, they leave.
I leave.

Am I like the talking clock? Or, perhaps this is like a kind of automated service which can be bought and switched on, used and then disposed of, as if I were a semi-sentient projection. An academic vending machine. I know not everyone thinks of me that way, but the system has already made its choice. What do people like me dream of when we go to sleep? Do electric lecturers dream of electric sheep? I decide not to go to bed for a while.

I turn on Radio 4 and listen to a documentary about shipping containers filled with millions of phone cases, transported via the Black Sea. Or, it could have been about an art installation featuring shipping containers. I'm not sure. I try to stay awake.

In the darkest part of the night, I fear I'm being possessed.

A phone case filled with floating, rose-gold glitter hung in the air above my bed. The glitter swirled and undulated inside the transparent plastic until it cracked and spilled onto the floor. The viscous skin of glitter spread and then stretched itself over a shipping container whose shadow lurked beneath my bed. A tsunami wave. A whale's mouth opens and all is consumed.

In the morning, I'm told my line manager has quit. Rumour has it they told senior management to fuck off in the very last meeting they had. I've got nine months left of my contract and the clock is ticking.

3
Spears

A permeation of dispossession
Queering our bodies
Still the tiger prowls
Possession[5]

From 'Zero' by Nikki Kilburn

You belong there. You do not own a single thing and you do not offer the world a single anything. You belong quietened. Hush, there is no need for that where you go, when you go, all quiet in the dark. Those arms are good for carrying, we will take them. As are those feet, for walking long, and fast, down deep. Further, still, in the black and the blue. Jawbone against my shoe, and your hair, shorn. Your stillborn smile. Your eyes will learn to read the faces and bodies of others: Instruction and Sign for clarity of purpose.

Your ears double the work of the eyes. They will hear songs you shall never sing. Light reaches you, its one purpose to brighten our reflection in the perfect mirrors of your eyes. These are your spears, your old ways and your custom, lying down for us, for years, and years, and years.

What do you think?

Sorry, pardon?

What do you think we could do to be more inclusive?

What. Do. I. Think?

The consumer product we are all peddling here, in this fine era of academia, is a kind of knowledge which we brand as the best, the most important, the most authentic and culturally significant, but whose origins lie in largely imperialistic ways of knowing and thinking. We are passing on patriarchal knowledge and perpetuating it, ad infinitum. It's so tempting right now to point at the screen and tell them we don't know anything. We know absolutely nothing.

There's a sequence in *Alien IV* where a version of the acid-for-blood alien has been cloned from Ripley, our ardent heroine. Part Ripley, part alien, the wailing clone is pulled through an airlock and sucked out of a window in slow motion, one fleshy bit at a time until only a few morsels of biological matter linger, before being flushed out with the rest of its remains. Ripley cries a bit, she really does, though it was her who threw the thing to its death. Ripley knew she had to do it, but nevertheless it still hurt them both – admittedly, one more than the other. In the end, Ripley was also part of the legacy of the parasite; it was in her blood.

Soon after the plague, there was a kind of purge which meant that every syllabus required more diverse examples and references. I had already done this for years, but now it was classed under a special term: diversity work. It had meaning where before it was just something I wanted to do because I cared. I mistook the acceptance of my care for acceptance of me. It was just the shuffle of the codes they were after. Suddenly, an extra role in your job description pops up. And another. And more! I became a representative of the new regime and that meant being responsible for changes that I had not signed up to and had no language for, because I had spent my whole life suppressing that language.

My parents were children of the British Empire and my great-grandfathers were colonials who married indigenous women from Burma and India. It is impossible to heal from the violence of those years and those ideologies through simplistic exchanges of one thing for another, swapping in a more culturally appropriate text and swapping out an 'inappropriate' one. These are steps on the ladder, but the ladder is long; it has multiple layers, it keeps moving like the staircase in *Harry Potter*. Would I give back the ceremony of an English cuppa, my father's beloved cricket, or the sugar in all the chocolate I consumed as a child, just to pretend that the British Empire did not exist? No, the British Empire penetrated my psyche as much as it penetrated my living bones, the great-granddaughter of colonial men who went out to the Bay of Bengal. What returned was not their legacy, but mine – my face, my voice, a child caught in time and also out of time, like Doctor Who spinning around her Empire-built Tardis.

This doesn't mean we should suffer indefinitely, but it does mean that a new language needs to be forged, and that takes time. You have to care first. I can't simply forget colonialism ever existed and I don't want to. I have to reconcile those parts of myself with the other parts. I can't throw all of it out of the airlock like Ripley did, because I was also brought forth from violence. So, effectively, there's no time to wrestle with any more nuanced complexities here – we are asked to stop feeling, to shut down anything emotional and just do the job. Levels of irony ensue. Levels with moving staircases in buildings no one uses, because this is all happening via Zoom.

Historically, very few academics from ethnic minorities have worked in the arts and this is also true of the student demographic. I had these statistics flung at me with force, multiple times via Zoom workshops. Here, I'm not an artist, or academic, or feminist, or teacher – suddenly, the thing I had buried in plain sight now becomes *the thing*. It's like those optical illusions where you look at a black and white image of a vase and then you look again and it becomes the silhouetted outline of two human heads facing each other. You can never really choose to see one thing or another; it's just something you see and then you can't unsee it. After all these years, the illusion shape-shifted. My second skin which clothed my hieroglyph bones had been shed, but not by me, and I was standing in my first skin, denoting my differences, invoking the uncanny dragon baby–Dragon Lady–Pocahontas. For me, these are just more layers, but the corporation wants to devour them. They eat them up. How can you be colonised more than once? Isn't there a rule about that?

Elsewhere, today, tomorrow, next week, last week, every night of the year, I sit reading a bedtime story to my youngest son. He puts his cold feet on my feet, warming them against my skin, under the covers of his bed. He leans over the book we've read many times before. He pokes me with his elbow, his knees, and I ask him to shuffle along the bed so that I can sit more comfortably. We settle again and I watch him fold back the pages of the book. He won't stay still for very long – he's like a stop-motion animation with all its jerks and sudden moves, static, then not static, leaping from one position to the next. Finally, he curls into a crescent in the bed and I'm able to see his features and his fingers gripping the book. I *see* him. I can see his long eyelashes as he looks down at a page. I block out the noise and concentrate on this time here, now. *Now.*

Throughout his childhood, he has had febrile seizures, around five in total. These come and go, but they happen fast. He contracts an infection and then he boils over, hot and sweaty, turning and jolting in his bed, or wherever he falls, as the seizure unravels him. The doctors say the seizures will pass in time and I'm sure he'll grow out of them, but for now I watch his every move. I follow him around at birthday parties like a feverish, unwanted fan at an Elvis concert. I chase him through rainbow-coloured soft play centres and tell him, in no uncertain terms, to avoid the slides. I know he has an increased chance of developing epilepsy in his later years. I watch him. I stay awake all night if I have to. It usually happens at night, when his immune system is likely to raise the body's temperature deliberately as part of its strategy to stop the virus attacking it. I get my phone and check it's charged. I check I've everything in my bag: keys, purse, phone charger. If he's starting to develop a fever, I get him up and we sit in the bed with the covers pulled back. I know for sure that these seizures, which arrived out of the blue, are my worst fear. The first time he had one, I thought he was dying. I'm desperate, but I hide it. I'm desperate, but I force my voice to sound calm. We read.

My son very much enjoys the simplicity of Judith Kerr's *The Tiger Who Came to Tea*. He's a little too old for this now, but we like looking at the pictures, especially the image at the end where the tiger is playing a flute. The idea of the tiger playing a tune always amuses me. He looks a bit like a snake charmer. That would make us the slippery snakes beguiled by the tiger's story.

Between holding my son and holding that book, there is such completeness, such love. I can do anything as long as we have each other. I can do anything. Nothing else matters. I create a force field around us and I tell him the magical ring by his bed will protect us both. My mother may be long gone, but I still have her jewellery.

How does it work? Do you charge it up?

Yes, like this. (I kiss the ring.) Like this.

Love you, Mummy.

I love you, too.

Maybe I should become a real writer, leave academia. But I'm scared. It's a life I've perfected for so long. I'll feed the institution some of me and in exchange, they will numb the pain. *Here*, I say, walking into the trap the snatchers laid centuries ago. Slowly, slowly, catchee monkey.

Why don't you share some of your lived experiences with us for our workshop?

4
Really, Really Interesting

In a way it was my fault, because I opened the lecture with a reference to Gustav Klimt. I wanted to tell the story of Salome and the transformation of the femme fatale throughout the history of art. I wanted to end with feminist interpretations of the female body and power.

Despite the plague and the constant chaos, it was a normal Monday. While the university fails to turn up the heating, letting draughts blow through its single-glazed Victorian windows, which they will never replace, I go down to the (colder) basement and switch on all of the lights in the auditorium. I'm still sweating from the walk I've had to do from the station to campus – nearly forty minutes at a breakneck speed because I missed the bus. I pat down my windswept hair and take a deep breath. And another.

Slide one: *Judith II (Salome)*, Gustav Klimt, 1909.

Slide two: *Salome with the Head of John the Baptist*, Carlo Dolci, 1681–1685.

Slide three: *The Feast of Herod and the Beheading of Saint John the Baptist*, Benozzo Gozzoli, 1461–1462.

Slide four: *Salome with the Head of Saint John the Baptist*, Lucas Cranach the Elder, *c.*1530.

Slide five: *Salome*, Titian, *c.*1550.

Slide six: *Salome with the Head of John the Baptist*, Michelangelo Merisi da Caravaggio, *c.*1609.

Slide seven: *Salome with the Head of Saint John the Baptist*, Artemisia Gentileschi, 1610–1615.

Slide eight: *Salome Dancing Before King Herod*, Georges Rochegrosse, 1887.

Slide nine:—

Someone wants to speak. A polite, respectful hand goes up, then a little higher, further and further until it separates itself from the shadows of the theatre and catches the corner of my eye.

There will be time for questions at the end and then we can discuss the lecture in our seminar groups...

A young male voice: *I just wanted to say something about the Klimt.*

His sentence ends on an ascending cadence so that it sounds more like a question than a statement, though of course it's a statement and the rising cadence is just a performance of civility and respect, because he wanted to talk and that's what is being asserted here.

Yes, perhaps in the seminar—

Is it true that the Nazis stole Klimt's work? Not the Salome, *but another portrait of a woman.*

This is a good question. He is referring to the portrait of Adele Bloch-Bauer, the 'Woman in Gold'. Yeah... Usually, I would never stop a lecture at this point, but now the question seems important. It's going off on a tangent, but best to give an answer. It's fine. I'm very glad the student isn't looking at their phone and is listening so intently, looking directly at me. Face to face. Just like the good old times. Except, this feels a bit intense. I don't think he's blinked once. I give him a little, encouraging smile. Perhaps this face-to-face thing will take a bit of getting used to again.

Yes, that's an excellent point. We might have more time to discuss Klimt in our seminars, but you're right, I can add a link to this week's reading from the Journal of Modern Art History *exploring this fact from the perspective of cultural studies and material culture. I'll add the link now… there we are. Thank you, what's your name?*

(Let's call him Perseus, the great beheader of Medusa).

Thank you, Perseus.

He continues: *Would you say that the Nazis were responsible for Klimt's success? They sponsored one of his retrospectives, didn't they… in Vienna? He wouldn't be as well known now if it wasn't for their celebration of his work.*

This is not where I wanted the lecture to go.

I think that's a fascinating thought, one which has been critically explored by a number of art historians, but we really must refocus on the central point of today's lecture, which is the femme fatale…

The Nazis also valued the work of Leni Riefenstahl, who became one of the most important female film directors in the history of cinema. They supported many artists and that legacy seems really, really interesting to me.

OK!

For the first time, under the dimmed lights of the lecture theatre, I noticed Perseus's appearance. Short, very short hair... no... a closely shaven head. And black leather boots. He is wearing heavy, studded boots and he has shorn off most of his blond hair down to a severe buzz cut. I can see the exact shape of his head. Tucked over the empty row in front of him (it's Monday morning) is a very long, black leather coat, but it's not really the clothing that sends the hairs on the back of my neck bolt upright. He has the softest, softest voice. He sits in the middle of the theatre and looks directly at me without blinking, not even once. He never appears to be conscious of the rest of the class, nor the fact that he is the only one speaking. The other students are looking at their phones or typing notes.

I just keep thinking that he has such a quiet, controlled way about him. His voice is almost indifferent, the tone is so even and centred. He carries himself as if he has power without ever needing to assert it. Have I just been away from in-person teaching for too long, I wonder. In the place where I have always felt comfortable and entirely at home, I now want to run. My body is preparing to run even before my brain has acknowledged this fact – my heartbeat is quickening and I'm looking for the exit. Except, I can't leave because it's not the end. I focus on my notes. It's like water off a duck's back, I keep telling myself. But all through the rest of the lecture, I can feel his gaze on me. My increasingly dry voice, then, though perfectly professional, carried a grazing, quickening thread of doubt.

After I finish the lecture, Perseus comes up to me and continues to talk me through his essay plans. He has never spoken in class before, only at this point, and he is particularly interested in *this* subject he plans to explore. He stands quite close to me, but not close enough for it to be obviously uncomfortable. He's tall, taller in the black leather coat and the platform boots with the silver studs. Everything is fine and then everything is not.

I walk past the lecture theatre and turn left into the bathroom. It's a low rasp at first. A small, huffy noise. I am very sick, very suddenly. Very sick. Head down. Legs light, throbbing. My nose is damp and my hair won't stay away from my face. I wipe my mouth and breathe out. I'm trying not to think of *Judith II (Salome)*, the head of John the Baptist, the shine on the platter, the robes, the hair, the little double chin of Artemisia's Salome and the pearl earring on Caravaggio's Salome – the dark, ghostly head on the plate she holds up to the heavens. The silver-studded boots. The smell of leather. The smell of leather is everywhere. I inhale

the hand sanitiser and the green paper towels. The NHS guidelines remind us to wash our hands for as long as it takes to sing 'Happy Birthday' twice (twenty seconds). Instead of 'Happy Birthday', I can't stop thinking about Wagner's 'Ride of the Valkyries'. I know I should probably try to stop that. I try not to think of anything but, obviously, the more you do that, the more the opposite becomes true.

I wipe my face and go over to the mirror. Someone laughs, but there is no one else in the bathroom. I run the taps and swallow tepid water. In the mirror, I've gone quite green. A deeper shade of lichen I had not seen before. An unfurling of oakmoss at my neck and the sensation of it travelling up my spine, behind my ears. My eyes are sparkling now like galaxies in a halo of black bracken. My body had seemed to expel a pile of betel nuts on to the floor. Burnished little seeds beneath my feet. They look like dozens of disembodied black eyes bouncing up and down to their own blinking beat. Before I can reach down to pick one up, I glance at the mirror and see that there are two crooked branches spinning from the back of my head. I feel the weight of them and their wrenching movement as they fasten to my hair, contorting and splitting into two distinct shapes, cracking and twisting into each other as they grow. They look just like a very thick crown of deer antlers. Staring back at the mirror, I finally recognise in that image something of myself and instead of fear and revulsion I feel a strange sense of wonder and relief.

Becoming animal, I felt the deep, pulsing of electricity through the overhead lighting and the thin strip of air coming from the air conditioning unit on the ceiling, the damp floor and the heat and noise coming from the corridors outside. Everything made a bellow and a scream.

I couldn't go outside so I stood looking at my own reflection, my head full of horns and trails of moss on my cheeks. I tasted chalk, bitter leaves, rosehips, lanolin, nettles, ferns. I felt a forest behind my eyes and a trickling of water, a spring running between Neolithic boulders far from where I stood; the wings of dragonflies beating over flowering waterlilies; droplets of rainwater; a wheat field in Somerset; Indian storm clouds; particles of ancient dust spreading out from underneath the curling bark of a peeling white birch. Every thought inside of me soared, spinning in the afterglow of these vivid sensations.

Then, my mind settled on one image, which kept on repeating as if someone was turning the handle of a zoetrope. It was a raven circling a field in slow motion. Wings rising and falling, disappearing gradually into even slower movements until they blurred into a sinuous cloud of black smoke. Sulphurous lines arched and spread like arrows. Perhaps this

was my only true desire. From such a height, it was possible to be entirely free. That lovely thought entered my sorrowful bones and then it left me.

I returned to where I was standing and I saw my feet planted on the floor of the bathroom, my body no longer obsidian-winged, weighted at its centre with a pounding urge for flight. Below me, the undigested betel nuts puckered and shivered. The betel nuts danced and danced, tapping out tiny rhythms on the floor. Out from them grew vivid, lime-coloured shoots which, in turn, produced rows of red poppies on the linoleum floor. I saw the poppies in the reflection of the mirror. My pupils changed from black to red, to copper, and then I fell through a chasm in time, or perhaps it was a cave. I heard a bugle, or maybe the distant cry of an elephant.

Someone lit a match inside the cave and asked me to enter.

5
Maha Giri

My mother writes a word on my back. Her finger is lightly tracing over me and I have closed my eyes so that I can concentrate. It's a game we've always played. She was teaching me how to write in Burmese and she thought that the best way for me to learn was to play a game every night with me, drawing letters on my back while I sat in front of her, brushing my bushy hair. I was maybe six or seven, unable to concentrate for long periods of time, but nevertheless willing to play this guessing game all night instead of begging for more of my favourite television programmes, or a bedtime snack of peanut butter on toast.

Have you finished? Is that it?

Wait.

I don't know what it is.

She poked me and I sat upright after slumping forward, fidgeting.

Come on. Think about it.

Don't poke me. Start again please, Mum.

Soon, she says, *we can start a few words.* She points at my back with her forefinger and she laughs a little.

This one is a bit funny, because it means something in English, too.

Don't make it too hard. I'll get it wrong again.

2

I don't know, Mummy. Is it a 'ta' or a 'ba' sound? It feels swirly. It's an 's', but it's lying down.

It's the word for the moon. The moon. Or the infinity sign.

What's infinity?

It means forever.

Like never stopping?

Yes, never stopping. Always, unending.

I heard my mother put her hands in her lap and I felt her body sighing. She yawned.

I'm a little tired.

But I want a story.

She seemed to 'rub out' the invisible sign she had drawn on my back and then she drew it again. I felt her finger loop over the curve of the word and back around itself. We were both thinking of little moons. Then, she leaned back against my pillows and asked me to sit next to her.

Nats are spirits who dwell in the mountains of Burma, especially on the sacred Mount Popa.

Nats…

There are two main types of nats: nat sein (she draws this word on my back နတ်စိမ်း), which are humans who were deified after their deaths, and all the other nats, which are spirits of nature (spirits of water, trees, and so forth).

Are nats good?

They can protect us, but they can also jump into human bodies and force them to do things they don't want to. We give them food so that they will be good. They take these offerings and then they leave us alone. A bit like when I give you a peanut butter sandwich.

I'll eat a whole plate of those for anything!

My mother didn't look at me as she spoke. She pointed out shadows on my walls and with each gesture of her waving figure, it was as if she was summoning an ancient book which had no pages, only vivid pictures moving from one image to the next.

One of the most worshipped of the Thirty-Seven Nats is Min Maha Giri. There was once a very powerful blacksmith named Maung Tint Tè who lived in Dagaung. He was so popular, people came from all over the kingdom to purchase his work and they loved watching him in his iron forge, taking molten metal and easily hammering it into anything they wanted. Some were envious of him, because he was a beautiful artist and he could sculpt anything he wanted from metal. His hands worked their magic and forged all sorts of things, including swords and decorations which hang in the holy places, gilded in gold. A few people thought he had holy powers and some were frightened of his special gift.

The King of Burma was so afraid of Maung's strength and skills that he sent men to spy on him. Perhaps he had been bargaining with the spirits, he thought. He listened to the tales his courtiers would whisper about the size of Maung's hands and the way he turned everything into wonderful shapes, moving the metal as if it were part of his own body. In a jealous rage, the king ordered his men to capture Maung and he was brought into the royal court with a rope around his hands and feet. The king demanded Maung to stop working, but he would not agree. Appearing to be kind and merciful, the king released Maung, but on the night after his return, Maung's house was set on fire and the forge was destroyed. Maung died in the flames, but his house burned for several more days. The king's queen, who was also Maung Tint Tè's own sister, tried to rescue her brother, but she never survived the fire.

Together, the brother and sister became nats, living in a tree in Maung's village. They cursed all the passers-by. The king ordered that the tree be uprooted and tossed into the Irrawaddy River, but it simply floated down to Bagan, where the king of that realm ordered that the wood of the tree be sculpted into statues of the two nats and placed in a shrine at Mount Popa, as he had been instructed in a dream. Mount Popa is very sacred, like Mount Olympus in Greece. Maung Tint Tè was given the title Maha Giri (Lord of the Great Mountain). The king organised a feast for Maha Giri at Mount Popa every year around the full moon of the lunar month of what we call 'Nayon'.

When my mother stopped talking, she seemed to still be deep inside of her own thoughts, as if she were dreaming while wide awake. She took off her favourite gold ring and kissed it. It was shaped like a band of branches woven together. She held it up to the light.

Look, this ring is made from Burmese gold. It represents part of the shrine at Mount Popa, like the statues of the nats carved from the tree.

My mother turned the ring in the light, where it shone and cast a warming reflection on her face. Her mouth opened but instead of words, I heard vines curling and spreading under the frame of my bed, tumbling over the carpet and up the walls. I saw my curtains shift and twist into thin branches where jacana birds nested in their folds. The room took on the appearance of a hollow inside a tree. It was dark and things moved all around. The water spilled out from the glass I always kept on my bedside table and it flowed into a river beside my bed. There were leaping fish and waterlilies, reeds taking root nearby.

A sacred bell rang out. Then I knew it wasn't a bell at all, but the clinking of a hammer on molten metal. The sound of a hammering iron in a forge. My mother's face became darker, fixing itself into a leaner, more angular shape and her lips became the colour of honeyed oak. Her hair was the deep colour of Burmese teak and her curls hardened into wood shavings all around her. Gritty dust rose up and settled at her collarbones; it danced near her cheeks and under her chin. Her whole face became a living nat.

Perhaps the nat had jumped into my mother's body, but it seemed to me also possible that it was my mother who had jumped into the spirit of the nat. *Clink, clink, clink.*

I fell asleep as layers of dust turned in the air and my mother, Maha Giri and his sister watched over me for all eternity, just as they watched over Mount Popa.

6
Being Seen

The walls of the cave were glistening and covered in stalactites. I tasted the mineral air and the moisture leaching from the salty, calcified rocks. Things moved and dripped all around me in slow, falling movements of precipitation from the jagged walls. Near and far, there were slippery echoes from the tunnels, which ran for what seemed like miles underground. Small, black, hooded creatures breathed in the darkness. There was a gathering swarm of movement and then I saw that there were hundreds of bats flying over me. They seemed to rip away the shadows, cracking open the hollow space and flooding it with light.

As daylight entered the cave, I saw a figure in what seemed to me like a pair of denim Lucy & Yak dungarees and Nike Air Max trainers with pink neon laces, whose synthetic fluorescence padded from side to side. The figure raised their arms and hummed a tune. It drew itself up from the stone floor and then I saw that it was a woman dancing. She looked the same age as me, but she had thick, braided hair and a tattoo of a lamb lying sideways across her chest. I didn't recognise the song she sang straight away; she seemed to be getting into the groove of some sort of funky beat, throwing her arms around and swaying her hips, raising and lowering her shoulders, clicking her fingers. After one more twirl, she sang the chorus, which I didn't notice the first time because of the bats. Her voice reached a crescendo and it was then that I realised she was singing Tina Turner's 'Disco Inferno'.

The woman appeared to be part of an imaginary dancing troupe. She looked like she was getting in line, forming a human train, clapping out the beats while she waited her turn again. She whooped and clapped, whistling a few times, before returning to the chorus and spinning around. She whooped again, making circular gestures with her fingers. She shimmied and threw back her head.

Excuse me, I said.

She turned to face me, but she was still jiving. She paused for a moment and then looked at me straight in the eyes. She sort of swaggered in a way that seemed to fill the whole of the cave and, as she swerved her body to the indifferent beats of the water dripping from the walls, I felt the energy of something friendly, an odd embrace. Her inscrutable features burst into a smile. Her movements began to slow down and she panted. One last whoop and she clapped her hands together. She leaned against the walls of the cave and moved herself around until she was comfortable.

When I dance, I don't want anything else. I just want to move, you know. I let my body be my guide. Dancing is the most potent form of self-fulfilment. People think it's liberating, but it's not that. It's not that. Do you know what dancing does to our bodies? It taps into our ancient selves, not the ones who danced around the fire and sang, but the entire cosmos, the Milky Way and all the moons too. All the moons! Eternal constellations of stardust just spinning over our heads.

The woman sat down on the floor and removed her trainers.

My feet aren't what they used to be. Now... tell me what you want to say.

I didn't know what to say. I was still staring at the woman's trainers and their drooping pink laces. It's true, I had forgotten how to desire. It seemed like it was an easy question, but the more I considered it, the stranger it became.

The trouble is, you don't know what you want.

How about I turn the one who shouted at you into a bat? I could do it... no problem. Or, take their soul and give it to the three-headed beast who lives behind the rocks, over there, further down the cave holes. Big egos taste like butter to him.

Or… you could have a moderately priced house near the coast and an endless supply of food and books. That's the kind of thing you like, isn't it? Have I got it right? I can never be entirely sure. You don't like lots of stuff, do you? That's hard for me, because stuff is easy. Come on, what do you really want? Don't say 'peace and health for all', because that's not my area.

I don't understand.

I'm here for you. I'm seeing you and this is it, here. You are being seen, fully and completely, unconditionally. My eyeballs… on you.

It was a sensation I didn't recognise. I knew this was a gift, but I didn't know how to accept it. Who are we when we are being seen, unconditionally, liberated from all the horrible injustices of the world? Who did I think I was and who could I become?

Becoming was rarely within the reach of my own vocabulary. Becoming was not something I understood. I was born grateful, or ignored, never entitled. I was always ready to beg, borrow or steal by any means necessary. I *borrowed*, but I did not *become*. I borrowed utterances, phrases, the way people held their bodies, syntactical elegance on the page. I stole things like umbrellas from common rooms or foyers. I wore other people's clothes, bought from charity shops long before that became fashionable. *Who could I become?* Hieroglyph bones always made inferior copies and I was never a real person anyway, more like a symbol of something old and other. Part of me felt undeserving, while the other parts were greedy for more nibbles and treats, open-mouthed for opportunity, serendipity, luck. My ancestral selves strongly believed in luck and I felt the weight of that, as if they were reading my fortune before I was even born, mapping out my life in accordance with some prophecy. It was them that cried for several days when I broke a bathroom mirror. It was them that split wishbones with my son at our Sunday dinners. It was also those parts of myself that made me go to fancy shops and spend all my money on designer perfume or earrings made by artisanal jewellers who lived in Folkestone. They clapped their eyes on shiny things and begged me to pierce my ears again so that I could wear even more of this treasure, especially while stuffing my face with crisps.

Who did I think I was?

It was simply easier to say who I thought I was *not*. I was not many things. I was not blonde. I was not rosy-cheeked with thin, athletic legs and hair you could come straight out of the shower with and just shake dry. I was not born knowing things like how to work a room or how to ask directly for whatever you wanted; I didn't know how to make connections and go out for drinks with people in order to become part of a network; I didn't know how to take other people's work and claim it as my own; I didn't know how to seek out money and how to acquire it, seamlessly; I wasn't good at pushing myself forward, or raising my hand if I had an answer in mind. I wasn't a lot of things. I could never be a leading lady, though you might see my silent, powdered face beamed from billboards like the ones in the Tokyo-themed cityscapes synonymous with *Blade Runner*. Put it another way: I knew I was not the sort of person who would push past others in a queue. I rarely complained. I rarely objected to anything and I always moved to the side of the road if I was in the way with, or without, a child in a buggy. These are just things I know about myself, but I also accept the fact that they do not affect my ability to be successful in life.

Who *didn't* I want to be?

I didn't want to be like my friend in customer service, let's call her 'Mrs Tiggywinkle', who became so stressed with her line manager that she developed a kind of locked-jaw syndrome (temporomandibular disorder) in which her muscles tightened and she couldn't open her mouth very wide without a searing pain. Mrs T's body refused to co-operate with her mind anymore, the mind that kept forcing her into that heinous workplace, and so it sealed itself shut – because, really, she wanted to scream and scream all day long and that would be a bad thing, so her jaw clamped, her own shop was 'shut' from then on and it resisted any impulse to open again. It was a rebellion she was forced to submit to. She was robbed of most of her speech. She sipped soup from a bowl. During this time, she had to think and stop apologising, agonising, anguishing. After weeks of self-imposed silence, she decided to quit the job, quit the feeling, and in that moment her body loosened, finally releasing her from jaw-aching purgatory. When that time came, all her body wanted to do was to let out a long sigh of relief – an open-mouthed, blissful sign of contentment – the very opposite of what Edvard Munch depicted in his painting *The Scream*.

I glanced again at the lamb tattoo on the woman's chest and then it became clear to me that I had seen it once before. It was a very particular image of a lamb copied from Zurbarán's seventeenth-century painting *Agnus Dei*. Just like the painting, the tattoo depicted a lamb lying on a slate table against a backdrop of eerie shadows. The lamb was still alive, but its legs were bound by string, its fate already sealed. In the painting, the lamb stares into an abyss beyond the frame, stupefied, fully surrendered to the facts relating to its imminent departure from the living world. I thought about how far I had come to being like the lamb, listlessly accepting my fate. Just how many pieces of rope had I set myself loose from? I wondered if the woman in the cave was the one who had caught the lamb, or perhaps she was simply the binding rope. Perhaps she was neither. Perhaps the woman seemed to be most like the rope-maker, someone entirely absent but crucial to Zurbarán's painting. What followed proved this to be true. She was not going to release me from fate – she was just going to herald a different one.

I watched the woman go back to her dance routine, awaiting my answer, but still nothing came out of my body.

Who could I become?

I saw myself like one of the glamorous lifeguards in *Baywatch*, swimming out to sea. In the distance were the shipping containers I had dreamed of many times before, the glittery phone cases and their shimmering trail of micro-plastics seeping into the ocean.

Who could I become?

Years and years ago, I had observed from afar a woman arriving at a Best Western hotel in Somerset dressed in a floor-length, black velvet coat with many large rings on her fingers. She spoke in soft tones and her straw-coloured hair was tucked behind her ears, long and celestial. She wore very little make-up and she was so calm, gentle and still. She was asking for the key to her room while her children waited in her glamorous shadow. I could smell camomile and rosewater. Or, at least I thought I could. Ever since I saw her, I wanted to be like her. I didn't really know why. It must have been her smell that drew me in. I wanted to be handed keys the way she was handed them. I wanted to stand in a hotel lobby and speak words which were merely superfluous, because things just came along into my hands and I was a queen. The weight of a solid brass key in my palms – it's true, that idea for me held its own tantalising allure.

Where would I live? I saw versions of myself living in Venice, Paris, New York. I imagined several lives like the ones I'd seen on social media, where every picture was taken in some opulent room with perfect table settings and candelabras. I saw myself with silky, straight hair that flowed like a beautiful mirror, just like the hair I had seen in hundreds of ads while I scrolled through Instagram. I knew these were things I never truly wanted, but the thought possessed me nevertheless. I was sure I didn't want to be like my mother or my father, because they were never really happy – was it shameful to want perfection? I didn't know who I could be in the future. I struggled with this question because, I knew, I was happiest being someone else, seeing through other people's eyes. I could not become one thing, because the pleasure was simply always plural. Plurality resonated with me, no, *within* me. More than anything, I wished for that plurality to evolve into something more; to bring me the strength I yearned for, which would elevate my voice and my spirit. Still, I held this answer in my body.

Let me help you.

The woman suddenly stopped moving after a while and pointed at my throat.

Let me help you.

She raised one finger and moved it sharply in the air, before making a gesture which appeared as though she was lifting something, as if she had a piece of string twisted around her finger and she was drawing it upwards, pulling it towards her like a hook.

Slowly, she dragged them from the well inside of me. She drew her finger down, unzipping an invisible seam, and then the words grew louder as they reached their summit. I felt my mouth agape and, as it remained open, voices spilled out which were not mine. Sometimes they spoke all at once and sometimes they argued amongst themselves. I heard voices in Irish, French, German and English, Burmese, Hindi and Spanish. They asked for the treasure of language in all its forms, verbal and nonverbal, and a vital absence within that – spaces of breath for the unsaid things, *for ourselves,* they said. They asked for community and kinship, to be fed properly with love and joy, strength to carry my body into the future, for our children and their children to come and, most of all, time for all of their stories to be told. They were simply asking to love and to fight hard for that love, to love and to protect, to prosper under the shade of the branches of all those flourishing stories, ever unfolding and reaching out towards the heavens: to *become*. There were a few whispers and sobs, and then the voices fell silent.

Water trickled backwards up the walls of the cave. Droplets of moisture rose upwards, instead of collecting in pools on the ground. Salt crystals grew into a gathering intensity of luminous peaks. I could taste these peaks in the air. Those walls in my mouth.

My mouth closed and then it suddenly opened again with an unexpected force which moved upwards, across my chest and through the back of my throat. My body lunged forward and I bent over. The woman watched me patiently but she did nothing. Then, she loosened her dungaree straps and pulled the fabric open so that it formed a kind of apron. I asked her what was happening and she raised one hand, indicating to me that I should wait. My face was bright red at this point and burning, sticky with sweat. That feeling when you know you are going to submit to the muscles in your stomach and you are your stomach and the back of your throat – nothing else. I tasted something like liquorice sours, and rounded, too, like the Chinese preserved plums I ate as a child. At first, they looked just like furballs, damp and slicked with saliva. Then, they moved and shook themselves out on to the floor. One by one, feathery things left my mouth and I saw the tiny faces of newly born birds. I spat out dark feathers. Little quills and scaly talons were scratching their way out of me. I looked ahead for any kind of answer, but the woman stayed very still. She didn't even blink. It passed and then I was surprisingly fine once the chicks were on the ground. I picked one up. It was so light in my hands. It chirped and shrieked before the woman came closer and picked them all up, depositing them into her apron-dungarees.

Like this, the cave became a nest.

I got you, I got you, little ones, the woman's voice sang, stroking the chicks, touching each one of their bobbing heads.

She told me the birds were good luck. She fed them worms, which also looked like little ropes, her bindings, which were tucked into the braids of her hair. Medusa-like as she stood there with these writhing bits of starling-feed gathered around the nape of her neck and around the tips of her ears, she hummed a tune and dusted off her dungarees, which were now covered in scraps of feathers.

The birds grew larger and then seemed to mature, in seconds, into young starlings. They launched themselves into the air and over our heads, spinning into a circular shadow, which contracted and expanded as if it had become the lungs of the cave and all was vibrating and attaching itself to this movement. I saw a black, knotted skipping rope coming undone and criss-crossing over itself, a murmuration folding into the wavelengths of the air, which I saw reflected in the woman's eyes before she spoke again. A double helix danced within the pupils of her eyes.

You forgot something.

She was right. I felt another solid shape writhe and move its way through my chest, my throat. It wasn't anything like a small bird. I leaned over, buckling under the pressure, and with one last wave of contracting motion, I seemed to spit out finally what looked like a fully grown white-footed Burmese cat. It came from deep within me. It was wet and slippery, but when it shook itself off, it was actually quite beautiful. It eyed me and then it eyed the woman, before disappearing under the frayed hem of her dungarees.

Huh. I didn't expect that, the woman said. *I thought it would be a stone or something. You must be very special.*

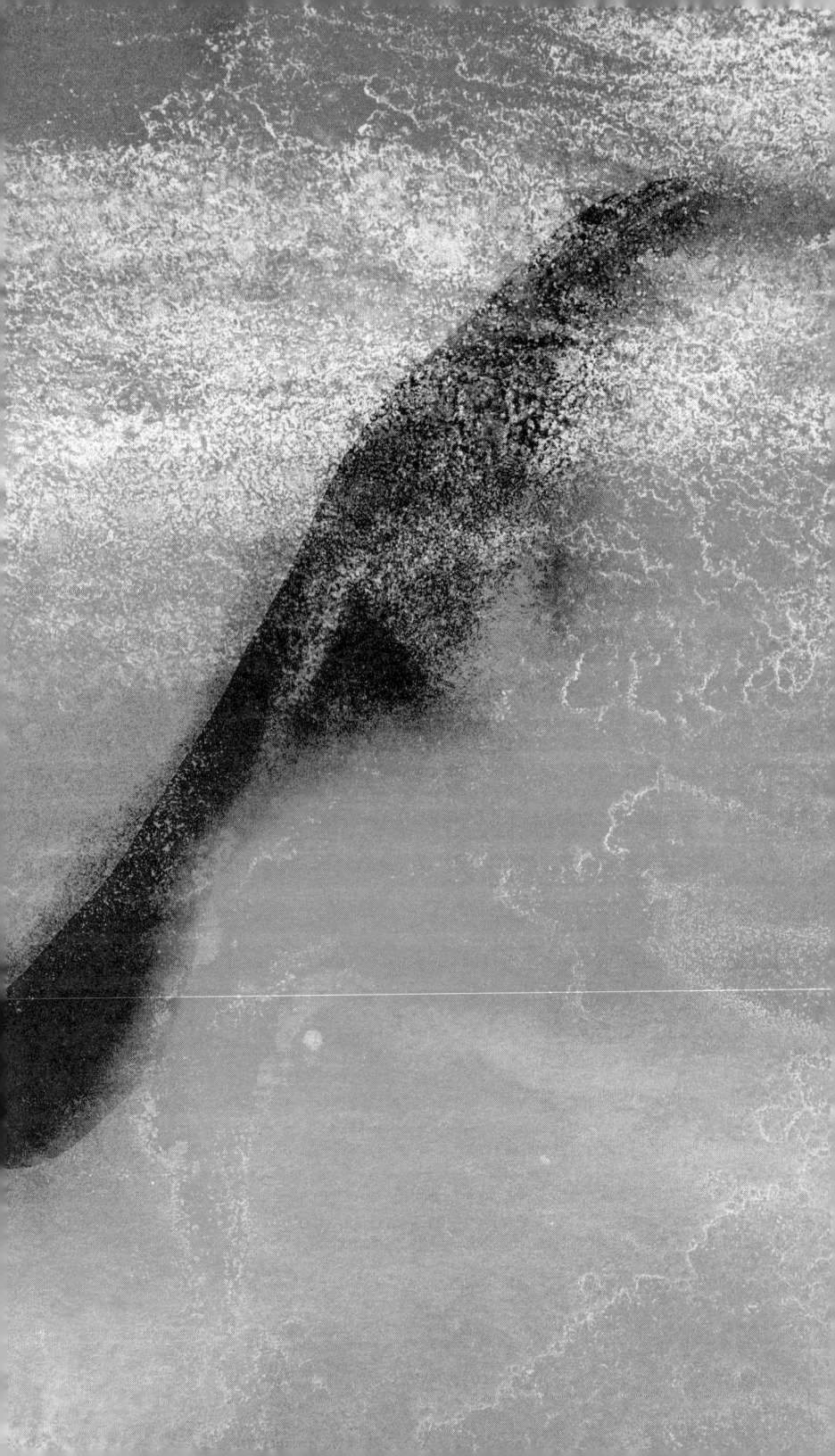

I saw the woman pull out something from her pockets. At first I thought it was a collar for the cat, but it turned out to be a brass coil for its neck, just like the ones worn by my Padaung ancestors. The woman slipped the coil over the cat's head.

Well, OK. I hereby announce that the cat represents... '*mystic ancestral power*'.

Unfortunately, I misheard most of this and it sounded to me as though the woman had said the word 'mistake' instead of 'mystic'. What was clearer to me was the word at the end, the word 'power'. I said something to the woman about Chris Marker and how cats are never on the side of power, but she just grinned and then, with one final, cackling shriek and a clap, she seemed to exit her body and her clothes fell to the floor in a pile. She had vanished, but the Burmese cat remained. It ran off into the cave tunnels, its pearly white paws padding off into the darkness.

The cave shone with a pale blue light, as if a series of overhead lamps had been switched on. The salt crystals glowed with a purplish hue. I was in an oceanic vortex, but there were no fish. *I'm going to drown here*, I thought. *The sea is entering the cave! The tide is coming in!* I waited, but nothing happened. Instead of water, I saw illuminated projections, scrolling information, numbers and names falling in waves across the walls.

Liquid symbols. Transforming signs. Constantly shifting lines of information, numerical patterns and codes. Below this, I saw data and URL links, web configurations and operating systems. I heard an electrical, high-pitched pulse.

From somewhere on the other side of the cave, I heard a voice tell me they were exiting the Zoom. I had nothing left to do except to log out.

7
Becoming

Hands on the keyboard. Eyes looking into the screen. Air filling my lungs, body settling. Breathing out. Becoming multiple. Something else slips out of the surface of the glass, the metal casing, the dust on the laptop, and suddenly I'm seeing through the layers of light, the frames within frames. I'm looking and I'm waiting.

A new temporal zone. A new flesh the colour of midnight. It's a slow movement in time towards the present. I feel myself looking with my whole body, seeing, suspended inside the colour of midnight. I have to search inside this darkness in order to see beyond the borders of things. I have to allow myself to float. Sometimes, I see space debris, an old satellite or the bisected glimmer of a meteorite. These things knock against me and, in their grazing movements, I feel something. I might remember what it feels like to be touched.

Gravity is the weight of my hands on the keyboard. The tips of my fingers and the veins on my knuckles. I can levitate between the keyboard and the screen. I can be the thin space between the dust and the glass, the mirror and the midnight inside of it.

Levitate.

Now, there is air between us. I'm upside down. I'm watching my hair dangle, my grandmother's gold bracelets at the tops of my arms, my earrings rolling sideways. I try to get back inside my body, but jumping back requires a certain kind of desire. I search for that desire, fighting the urge to sit on the edge of existence and watch the stars. I can become a gathering wind, a tremulous breeze, a cough in the dark. I can summon a spinning palace of winds, but first I must exhale. Wind carries itself. Wind is an alchemical becoming.

Look carefully and you will see storm clouds behind my eyelids, a raincloud about to burst. My ancestors tell me to remember light and heat, water and air. We cannot exist without these elements and our bodies are made of the earth and sky. These ancestral mothers have fed me and their mother's milk will never have its genetic equal in the metaverse. I still carried that trace of mother's milk inside of me as I fought to feel whole again, to be returned to my body.

Another 'mother' keeps entering my mind. I can't stop thinking about a piece of artwork called *The Artist Is Present*. In
2009, the Serbian performance artist Marina Abramović sat
at a wooden table across from a single chair at New York's
Museum of Modern Art. Abramović did this for 700 hours,
eight hours a day over nearly three months, while members
of the public came to sit with her. Nothing interrupted the
performance, not even a break for the bathroom. People
came and went. Some participants took things seriously and
sat, composed and quiet opposite this world-famous artist,
listening to her breathing. Others laughed. Some cried.
Some felt nothing and walked away, as was their right, as is
anyone's right to choose what to do. Marina sat and sat and
sat and sat. Her face became a screen. As time opened up for
the sitter and the one opposite them, all became measured
by, and was relative to, the present moment that existed
and only that. Without words, or actions, face to face, they
shared the moment and opened themselves up to its deep
energy. Transmitting and receiving energy at the same time,
the artist became the present.

When was the last time you really looked at someone?

I often thought about that clever bird, Marina, as I sat
in front of the screen in my bedroom. Sometimes, I couldn't
stop thinking about her. Had she known about the time that

was to come, when all we would do was look at each other for hours and hours, over and over, but in a way that totally failed to make ourselves, each other, present? I stayed still, sitting in the same place for months, while I met with hundreds of faces, strangers coming and going, all on the same dust-speckled screen. *It's fine*, I kept saying, trying to avoid complaining as I felt the workload weigh heavily on me, even when it carried itself inside my weightless, invisible voice. I was a medium of sorts, a spirit guide, but even the best mediums know when to stop and turn on the lights. I kept going. I never even stopped for water. The light was already on – a rectangle that became a transmitter, a battery, a crystal ball.

I tucked my legs under a blanket and rubbed my temples with my forefingers. Regularly, I put down a cup of tea and then forgot about it; a ritual I had performed countless times, as if the tea was never for consumption but rather to mark a point in time when the séance started.

It's fine! It's absolutely fine! It's not like I'm going down the mines. It's not like I'm going down the mines. It's not like I'm going down the mines.

But it's also true that my ancestors were inextricably linked to Burma's extractive industries. My paternal grandmother, Parquala, came from the ruby region and my paternal grandfather worked for the Burmah Oil Company.

It's likely some of them did go down the mines and if they weren't down the mines then they suffered anyway, deeply affected by the industrial and economic conditions that arose from colonialism's obsession with extraction. Others 'went down the mines' so that I would not have to. A quick search on Google tells me that there are at least 708 metal mines and 345 non-metal mines in Burma today.[6] I suspect my paternal grandfather only married Parquala because she owned land with rubies sparkling underneath it. As for me now, I can't help feeling like I'm in some sort of telesales situation. I've got my earphones in and I've got just the one commodity to supply here: me. *Hello/hello/hello/hello/hello/hello/hello/ hello/hello/hello/hello/hello/hello/hello/hello/hello/hello.*

I ushered them through. I accepted them. I *invited* them in. My colleagues hardly ever broke their 'vow of silence', talking *at* me, but rarely telling me anything of any value beyond its professional use. The students who did choose to turn on their cameras had to 'face me in the Zoom'. Face to face, eye to eye, but yet not really, nowhere near the real thing. Those particles of light, those transmissions that passed through the wireless network and the router in my living room, they spoke and we met each other in the hall of mirrors. We spoke and we invoked – what? – the idea of *connection.* Some of the faces were self-conscious, checking their appearance and moving their hair as they spoke; some said nothing and I watched as they thought of things to say; there were shy glances, awkward grins, the biting of lips, the open-mouthed spectre of anxiety or fears left unspoken, incessant sniffs and intermittent coughs, sips from mugs of tea or coffee. I had hope in my heart for every single one of them. I kept the fires lit.

No one ever cried, but there were countless haunted expressions of despair or loneliness which I could not overtly acknowledge or respond to, even though we both knew they were there. But I had to try to help. I had to do something. Like Marina, I received the energy of the attendees and transmitted thoughts and knowledge to them through the exchange of learning. I received all of their energy and it filled up inside of me like a swarm. I carried the lovely smiles, the tentative glances, the hopes, the niggling doubts. But, of course, it was a kind of possession which I had offered myself up to; it was literally a contract I had signed.

The swarm
     mutated into a gathering of stones
          which lined my insides and
               clustered into broken things
                    inside my hieroglyph bones.

The weight and colour of sea-glass adrift inside of me, like the stuff I used to collect down by the beaches in Cornwall. *Flotsam and jetsam.* Present, I performed something which seemed complete, while the conversation fractured and I tried to gather everyone up with my voice. I thought I was a spirit guide, but then it dawned on me I was more like a multiple socket power point, a USB charging cable with a pink neon lead (my preference). Whatever.

I could moderate the tone, dial it down. This was compounded by the personal interactions I had with family and friends, as well as colleagues, outside of the institution, which occurred on FaceTime and everywhere else, but always, always on a screen. I personally could do without looking at my face while I try to think. Looking back at my own face, I try to do my job. Looking at my own face feels like I'm also speaking to me. Perhaps I am. Projections within projections.

I'll catch you.

It was like trying to catch the wind. I tried to catch them all. I tried to save them. I was so certain, reliable. I learned how to transmit versions of myself, a monument to knowledge. All I had to do was to communicate confidence, which I hoped they would receive and manifest for themselves.

I took off my feet and my hands, passing them over in a box for safekeeping. I dreamed of sand dunes and heather catching fire on the moors, the taste of rock salt and the stinging astringency of sap from the pine trees near my house. I sat and watched faces appear and disappear as if they were differing phases of the moon. Yet all that energy, its ebbs and flows, wouldn't empty itself at the end of the day. Instead, it tried to jump inside my body forever. My ancestors waved sticks and shouted, because they were already inside me and they would not leave. They peered at the faces on my screen and they told me to get back into my body and to stop floating.

'S T O P   F L O A T I N G,' they shouted, from the bottom of the well inside of my body. In desperation, some of them removed the brass coils from around their wobbly necks and used them as anchors to weigh me down, to stop me leaving my body. They tried to catch me with these brass rings.

In the end, they resorted to pinching my face, scratching at the skin just below my right eye and my lower lip, as they had done before. Parts of my face trembled and went into tiny spasms, mini earthquakes threatening to fissure the surface of my skin. I knew then that my ancestors were attacking whatever was trying to get in. A casualty of war, I saw myself fall backwards and a thick pulse of movement ran through

me as they pulled me in all sorts of directions. I tried to hold on to something solid, but I could not move, subjected to the whip of their brass rings. I fell back against the carpet and saw the ceiling above me. In the corner of the room, I saw a spider's web, Dali's dripping clock faces, scissors criss-crossing above my head and an upside-down chair just like the one Marina had once used, now empty and weightlessly rotating about the room.

I had left my body, but my ancestors tried to grab me from the ether and stuff me back in. They wrestled with the thing that tried to enter my bones, but as they fought, they got seriously confused. Then something twitched and it wasn't me. Something took a sharp intake of breath, but it wasn't me. My ancestors were supposed to help me become present again, but instead their coils caught my youngest son and made his body shudder and jolt in his bed upstairs. They set something off deep inside of him and it wouldn't stop. I tried calling out to him, but nothing happened. He was gone. Again. His eyes were wide open. My eyes were wide open, but neither of us were there. *Breathe, come on…* I say to him. *You've got to breathe.* Nothing, I hear nothing and I know he's holding his breath. I don't know what to do. He's still holding his breath. I know he can hear me. He listens, he listens somewhere. I watch his mouth move silently, widening with each convulsion. He speaks to the celestial world beyond, the place only he can see behind his eyelids.

> A febrile seizure is like a hundred alarm bells
> after midnight,
> blue lights across our fields.

My ancestors were still winding their coils around us. Bound by the lasso grip of these brass halos, held inside their ribs of dazzling light, we were somersaulting through golden rings. Our bodies caught on the battlefield – his body, my body, an alternating pressure between us. And all the while we tried to leave, but instead we found ourselves leaping together into the things above our heads, shuffling through all the turns of the objects which were levitating above us – the chair, the scissors, the melting clock faces.

His cheeks are on fire. It was me who should be burning. His cheeks, his cheeks! My ancestors had made a terrible mistake. My son is only little. Surely, he can't keep withstanding these shocks to his system? What should I do, what could I do, in this state of emergency? Which knowledge could I rely on here? I pray for this to end. I press my face against his and tell him I am everything he needs me to be.

In the corner of the bedroom, I see that the Fates have turned away and I call out to them with fury in my veins. They say something like, *Sorry, this isn't our area. Have you tried using the phone?*

I have to show my son the way out. I make a map of my body. I make a compass of my heart. I shake myself loose from those brass coils and watch them shrink into glimmers revolving in the darkness. I get back into my body and place my feet firmly on the floor.

Gravity.

Now, I won't let my son go. I won't remove my hands from his body. His curling weight against my chest, his hands in my hands. His sweaty hair between my fingers, damp and knotted. I carry him. I carry him. And in my arms, he wakes. He settles into being again, into presence, the *nowness* we share together. He takes his time, but he comes back to me, like he always does. His presence – the most beautiful thing in the world.

Love like this,

an overwhelming

contagion.

Later in the hospital, a nurse brings us a plate of toast and strawberry jam, which my ancestors devour, along with an anaemic block of vanilla ice cream and a polystyrene cup of tea with three sugars. I have nothing to say to them. I stroke my son's forehead and kiss him there. He takes what is left of the toast and chatters away to the nurse, his body now a familiar set of clockwork rhythms. Landing back in my body, our bodies, we hold hands and I'm sure that this time I won't let him go. I'll not leave my body if he doesn't leave his; at least, that's what I say to myself, what I say to my ancestors scowling round the corner. They think I cannot see them, but I see everything. Their little faces, sheepishly watching from afar, have half an eye on the jam that I smear on more rounds of toast and half an eye on my hands still shaking as they pass through my son's thick waves of hair.

Occasionally, my son's head jerks and I examine his every move. *Are you OK? Are you all right?* I say. *Look at Mummy.* It goes on like this for as long as it takes for me to feel safe. I have to hold on to myself holding on to myself – me holding on to me, holding him, that unending ladder of self-care again, which was also care for him and for all of us who lived together in this one place under so many stars, suspended between what I could only describe as an enormous gathering of brass coils.

Are you staying? May as well run the tests while you're here, the nurse says.

My head turns and I look at her. I give her a smile and then I nod so that there can be no misunderstanding. I'm not going anywhere, because my hands are still shaking. If the nurse thinks I'm leaving, she's got to be fucking joking. The Fates agreed. After all, they loved hospitals the way some mortals loved all-inclusive holidays with the breakfast buffets stacked with waffles and ham the colour of freshly plastered walls.

Back in my body, I saw things differently for a while. One day, three girls came to meet me on the Zoom. I had known these girls for some time prior to the pandemic and they came along smiling and enthusiastically asking questions about their assignments. They had heard me give a public lecture on Hilma af Klint's mysticism and had a few questions about their group presentation on feminist cinema and representations of enchantment. Good for them! They had started following me on social media and they asked me for further reading, as if each bibliographical reference was a Ferrero Rocher they could gobble up. I recognised their hunger and gentle trust in the world, and that recognition brought back to life something inside of me. I could almost taste the silky flavour of knowledge that I had once known. The girls looked at me with their open faces, attentive, thinking without the bitter aftertaste of cynicism that comes with age. They were like tulips in bloom, pretty heads popping up from the spring earth, unaware of the looming presence of the secateurs, which would inevitably prune their wind-shaken, wilted bodies once the autumn arrived. I basked in their giddy spectrum of new growth. My only desire was to give them more light.

Self-knowledge is a kind beauty, isn't it? It restores. As I listened and saw the wonder on the girls' faces – the true wonder of learning something new and loving it, because it helped them to understand how they saw the world – I felt someone hand me back my sense of hope and belief. For once, I wanted something and I wished for this time to never end. I didn't bother putting my earphones back in, so I turned up the volume and leaned back. At that point, instead of the sensation of possession, I had the distinct feeling of being poured back into my body again. New thoughts emerged and we found ourselves laughing and talking as if we were back in our seminar room, listening to the air conditioning and the broken projector switching itself on and off. This new moment, this present one which existed only via screens, was anchored in our past lives and past experiences – it was soothing to me, a rarity. They were as excited and engaged as they had always been. The beauty of it was that it was their discussion of enchantment which had broken my own spell.

Once, an old friend, a lover in fact, had come to sit opposite Marina – the German performance artist Frank Uwe Laysiepen, also known simply as 'Ulay'. In this moment, time and space jerked around a bit and tried to settle into a new shape. Like Marina and her former lover staring into each other's eyes, these students brought about a new sensation, which was also old – it leapt into existence in a way that other interactions did not. It was a trespass across timelines and that made it revolutionary, a revelation.

Which present were we in now and could the feeling extend beyond this to some eternal space in our hearts, or would it be lost forever? Which things would be remembered and when would those memories surface again in another life, other lives, as the girls grew and carried parts of me with them? My body tingled and my voice hit new notes of excitement, curiosity, admiration.

The familiar faces of those girls brought with them the memory of my body and my presence before it had been transmuted into absence. Plainly, it brought joy. This extended to friends and people outside of work who just dropped by to say hello or share a cup of coffee with me online. Sometimes, we simply sat with each other and watched films or weird, experimental art together. We laughed at things we didn't understand. We constructed a new way to encounter each other and share our time. I knew this wasn't real, but it felt like love and I accepted it.

I turned a tarot card over, or perhaps it was a new window opening on my screen, or a saved picture on my phone, and then I saw myself multiplied, but none of them were me. I saw myself in the online lectures, the seminars, the tutorials, the public readings and the online conferences. I saw images of the images taken as screenshots during these events and I circulated those again on social media. I sent updated website links with pictures of myself and I shared stories on social media where I had been added and mentioned. I liked and unliked things that I didn't really like or dislike, but felt obliged to acknowledge.

In this chain of possession and containment, I began to feel something separate itself out from between the spaces of those pictures and the body I occupied in the *face-to-face* world. I realised I was not in any of the pictures I had shared or viewed. I was on the other side of those pictures and I was multiple while they were singular. Such strange singularity in so many copies. I was still there looking out at the world with my hieroglyph bones.

Out of the corner of my eye, I caught sight of the view from my bedroom window. There were a few clouds darkening over the fields, threading themselves together against a kind of padding light, which trailed into vanishing recesses in the sky. From under these curling lids of dappled whiteness, a faintly perceptible gleam of moisture revealed itself in their hollowed crests. Something seemed to turn a corner in the atmosphere, a dipping in the levels of sound, a widening of sensation as I watched crows scattering from the ash trees and the sessile oaks. Then, I heard a pattering of tiny drums on the wooden floor and on the single-glazed pane of the sash window. Scraps of air and light intertwined and danced on the ceiling, while something shook all the door handles and the bricks in the chimney. An invisible hand seemed to whip the air just in front of my eyes and then there were flashes of brightness. A low synth bass and then the emptying of the sky as it fell through the floor in ribbons of moisture, colourless angles of sound.

It was raining, but it was not just outside, it was *inside*, falling, falling, in perfect lines within the walls of my bedroom. The water, the water, everywhere and here, and here again, summoned, it seemed, by some invisible rainmaker. Inside, everything was shining. The dog-eared pages of my books started to curl and the threadbare pink sheet on my bed deepened in colour as it soaked. Torrential rain ran off the mantelpiece and slapped itself against the keys of my computer. Droplets formed on the top of an old wooden chest of drawers and grew into great circular pools the size of dinner plates. The old guitar, which lived in utter neglect in a corner, sent its own discordant song about the room as its strings were plucked by the liquid lines of the downpour. A slow, steady beat of dripping upon all of my possessions – an old hairbrush, a pair of silver hooped earrings and my grandmother's Indian bracelets on a bedside table, an empty mug or two, shells from Exmouth beach, my eldest son's old art project in the shape of an Egyptian canopic jar – all the things I had stared at for months as I glanced up from my computer and tried to anchor myself in the reality of their weight and texture. Back then, I concentrated on the presence of these objects as I felt all of my own matter leak out of me and, quite simply, dissolve into nothingness. Now there was no line drawn between myself and the outer world; we had simply coalesced into this odd yet beautiful shape. Bone-deep in feeling, I was no longer in exile, for the elements had brought me home.

I tasted saltwater on my tongue and at the back of my throat. The river inside my bedroom, my bedroom inside the river. I placed my hands on the windows and, at my wrists and the joints of my fingers, I felt the growing intensity of the rainfall, which also sounded like white noise. Outside, the rain continued and I could see the lanes were filling up with rainwater and stray, clustered ends of cowslips and dog roses, which were being carried, upended, through the shivering ditches, passed along the foamy streaks of the wash. A dog walker darted towards the broad shelter of a sycamore tree. Impatient blackbirds, as they always are, headed for the skies, chattering in what sounded like annoyance at the sudden alteration in the otherwise clement weather.

Like those blackbirds, I knew I wanted flight. But then I also desired other things (because I had finally remembered what it was like to desire). There was an urge to sit on the tips of the trembling branches of the ash trees by the house, to enter into the trickle of feathery light from behind the hedgerows, to roll, push, scrape my fingers along the miniature maps of lichen and the dimpled carpets of moss, to press deeply into their strange, plangent patterns. I longed for the feeling of running water at my feet. I wanted to feel the uneven, granular levels of clay soil in my garden and I wanted to watch the rain collect around the hem of my skirt. Most of all, I wanted to feel the wet grass. It was not long before the smell of petrichor entered the air and wafted into my room, as thick and dense as any perfume.

BECOMING

I ran downstairs and opened the door. I stood on the lawn, avoiding old shuttlecocks and dimpled tennis balls, bits of coffee grains and the gravel, which had migrated from the driveway. I stepped forward and I opened the garden gate. I walked outside and then I kept going until I reached the river. I rolled up my skirt and I stood by the river's edge. I let the river reach my knees and then I walked into its light-flecked, burbling flow. Now, waist-deep, I navigated twisted, fallen logs, which had made small islands within the river's body. The logs nudged each other, as if drawing to a close some clandestine conversation, and then casually slipped around a corner of the river, past the smudged reflection of a herd of grazing Red Ruby cows and the looming, sprawling shadows of blackberry bushes, heavy, laden with fruit. As I watched these sinuous, charcoal sketches on the water glint and sparkle with life, I came to understand how I had not been, for a very long time, present in the living world, merely floating parallel to it, stolen away by mirrors, screens within screens.

I had been teaching online and all the while the seasons had changed and I had barely noticed. I had forgotten the sun. I had forgotten the moon, too. Most of all, I had obscured the memory of the floods where I lived. I had witnessed them so many times before, but only now a memory returned to me. My youngest child being carried through water which reached my knees, his legs knocking against my hips, his hands gripping my shoulders, as I held on to his wriggling body. Back then, I would often put on the brakes of my son's buggy and abandon it in the lane as we trod onwards. Out there, the sly, conspiratorial current of the river sounded, binding itself to every living thing; the torrent of sequential noise coming closer, closer still, as the rain came and broke the flood defences.

The almost mute yet palpable sound of the water running off the hills in the distance and spilling into everything, higher and higher as things rose to the surface and swirled pathetically near the drains, which overflowed and clogged. Water depth gauges and warning signs. The sage colour of my old Dunlop wellies taking on a luminous quality as they succumbed to the soaking. The weight of the water against my ankles and calves. A dragging sensation – was it me or was it the water? We pulled each other through the depths. My booted, lower legs disappearing into the murky water as I stepped into it and inched forward, this slip-slap-slapping sound becoming a corollary of place, of home, as all came undone in the lanes off an A-road in rural England, the exact spot where I hid myself away and gave my voice and face to spectres on a small screen in my bedroom. I wondered, perhaps it was me, after all, who had brought the downpour. Often, I would look out from my bedroom while I taught and wished for anything and everything that would bring what was outside *in*. Contact. Communion with the living.

There were once deep vibrations and movements in the air, soundwaves I had forgotten. Merlin, Apache and Chinook helicopters, low-flying Eurofighter Typhoons and F-35 jets would often make their tornado-like appearance across the flatlands of the farm. How fast they flew over the rooftops of the hamlet where we lived. Such coruscating, nerve-jangling roars across the barley and wheat fields. These wrenching cries, which, combined with the floods, made me think I was living in some kind of peripatetic zone of utter conflict and devastation. I thought of my parents, who had endured such times in Burma and India. Yet still I loved the place. I tried not to fall, though I knew I was knee-deep, heart-deep, breath-deep.

I felt the wind on my face pulling at my hair and blowing across my temples. This quiet grace, this weather-bound, weather-worn feeling, it brought me back home to the lanes and far away from the blue screens I had been consumed by. I was straddling the very borders of time and space again. I saw before me the opening up of all of existence unfolding in the lanes near my house in Devon. I was no longer caught inside

the simulacra mirror-world of the non-living, the undead of late capitalism and its insane, annihilating logic.

I listened closely to the somersaulting currents of air still tumbling through the hazels and the sycamores as the afternoon light kissed the narrow veins of emptiness between their branches. Some kind of tender feeling for this place returned, rising from the depths of the furrowed land. Once and for all, my body yielded to this strange yet familiar song. Here in the valley, a homecoming. Here, a blessing. The sweep of the lane, which carried itself down towards the old barns where lambs were kept with their mothers, crossed itself over my heart as if it were a sacred thing. I stood and stared at the dusky colour of the crumbling bricks of the barn, uneven with subsidence; the splintered, rickety joints in the old window frames; the arch of the entrance thick with the stench of damp straw, muck and fleece. Elemental memories, the very skein of life, they had their own way of working themselves into your bones, from your head to your toes.

These things, which all belonged to the world beyond the square of my bedroom window, they were like scraps of old hymns I had learned by heart over the years, whose ascending chords, sometimes ragged, sometimes glorious, revealed to me in their purity a kind of love I had never known before. Even in their bleakest incarnations, when the weather turned and everything withered to scaled-back versions of themselves – line drawings stilled within rivers of snow and ice – their repeating scales exhaled in perfect intervals across the valley. I had discovered a new reality, which soothed the sorrow in my hieroglyph bones. I honestly thought I could be held forever within those charged intervals of light and song. And then that peace was stolen away from me.

A flock of geese passed over the rooftops of the outbuildings and disappeared over the valley, as they always did this time of year, the sky colouring, darkening under their wings. I sought shelter under the archway of the barn and watched the rain pass through the hedgerows and over the cattle grid near where I stood. At one of the metal farm gates, which yawned back and forth, I caught sight of a figure standing there, shawled and solemn in the breeze. She had always been there, though I had forgotten about her, along with everything else. My eyes lowered for a moment, afraid she would see the look on my face, the shame I carried in my chest.

All this time, she had been waiting with a prayer – Saint Sidwella. She held in her body the water and the land; no, she *was* the water and the land. Her head turned slowly towards

the south of the river and I saw, then, quite clearly, the back of her neck, which held no trace of wound nor bruise, not even the faintest of scars. She was whole again.

There she was, her profile in silhouette as the clouds behind her head shuttled and spun across the sky in drifts of whiteness. Time slowing down. The past entering the present. A rolling mist emerged from her mouth and encircled her head as she moved forward. She turned to smile at me and then I saw her face properly, lovely as it was, and I realised she was just a girl, young enough to be my own daughter (oh, how I had once longed for a daughter that never came). I raised a hand towards her, not quite a wave, but an acknowledgement nevertheless. In return, she lifted a single, slightly arched finger and pointed towards a knot of movement in the river, near its rasping, overflowing banks.

Sidwella held out her hands, but she did not offer me water, for there was enough of that already. With her hands, she made a shape that resembled a bowl. I knew what to do.

I cupped my palms together and gathered up the running water from the river. Like this, my hands became a vessel. The water turned warm and began to smell like freshly cut ginger and ground pepper from my mother's kitchen in Hayes. Steam rose from this broth. It was then that I gave my ancestors *hin* soup and I told them I loved them. I took what I could from the water and then I gave them dry shrimps, cellophane noodles and their favourite banana cake transformed from a wedge of silted soil. I told them I would bring them more. I swallowed the soup in one gulp.

The water sung, the water spoke, while my thoughts entered its flow and tipped language into air, into moisture, into movement. *I'm sorry*, I said. *I'm sorry it had taken me forty years to return the love I was born with.*

I'm sorry for feeling ashamed of your beautiful faces, your accented words which sailed inside my body for so many years, adrift inside these waters. I'm sorry for pushing you away as I pushed rice away and hid it down the side of the sofa when my mother's cooking was too spicy; for wishing my hair was lighter, my whole body lighter, so that I might be lifted up, away from you; for carving myself from your bones and never being grateful for the movement and light you provided; for denying the bravery and knowledge you set, like gems, into my eyes, so that they might better see the world; for taking your spears and turning them into dust so that I might live for a decade, or two, in the house of your masters.

I brought them a garland of jade, dredged from the many stones at the bottom of the river.

Forgiveness.

POSSESSIONS

In the city, another miracle occurred. Joni Mitchell appeared under the mural of Saint Sidwella and, on the wind, she graced the air with the opening lines from her song 'River'.

8
Golden Rings

I spend two years, more, doing interviews online. You shouldn't ever leap from the plague-fuelled frying pan into the fire. But you can, I learned, sit in two frying pans at the same time – I did interviews across the day, one after another. *Hi! Hi, nice to meet you.*

While I tried to remain tethered to the feeling of wholeness, I searched for job after job, but all I ever got were rocks and compacted bits of dirt, mere scrapings from the earth's core. I was at the level of the ground and it seemed to me as if it was only other people who got to see the stars or comets flying across the Milky Way. Permanent jobs.

I'm no longer entirely sheltered inside my own home, a place where I should feel safe. How would a crab feel if its shell was so permeable that it let in all sorts of intruders rustling under its smooth carapace? An invisible door opened up in the walls of my house and now I can never close it again. They come through for all sorts of reasons, but the worst is when I've invited them in for the sake of a job interview. I won't see these people ever again, yet here they are. Here they bloody are.

Buddhists use the word 'door' in connection to our speech, as well as our bodies and minds. What sort of door was opening here and was it for me, or for *them*?

After my contract ended with the university with The Tower logo, I made a career of doing interviews. This, too, was a kind of possession. At first, I felt nervous. Pacing about the room, checking the Wi-Fi, googling the names of the panel, if they were provided. Of course, I've not got the luxury of a home office or a spare room. I do every single job interview in my bedroom, away from the children, who must observe a monastic silence every time I 'go on'. Their Buddhist ancestors are extremely proud. You can hear a pin drop. (Or was it their plates falling off the side of the armchair?)

Before I begin, I walk past the dishes piling up in the sink, take the clothes out of the washing machine, wipe away crumbs from the worktop and those lurking inside the little drawer that slides out at the bottom of the toaster. I push some bills aside. Hoover. Bleach the bathroom sink. Brush the dog's white, wiry coat. Pluck a dead spider from a corner in the hallway. Put the clothes back into the washing machine. Pick a bra, a pair of knickers and everyone else's underwear off the bathroom floor. While I do this, I have to think about what is going to happen. My answers. My tone. I get caught in this vicious loop throughout countless interviews. I don't like it at all. The whole thing is airless. I feel panicked in my own private space. I can't breathe. I can't breathe. I can't phone anyone, I don't have anyone. What to do? I have to imagine something new. I have to turn that space inside out.

I hold out my hands and the room shrinks to the size of my laptop, which, in turn, folds into smaller dimensions between the movement of my fingers and the modulation of the words getting caught in my throat. I concentrate on the squares of light from the windows and the shape of their frames, their corners, the way that the clouds make vanishing archipelagos of light out of the nothingness over there, far, far from here. I make a habit of watching those squares, attending to their sacred geometry. Or perhaps I'm simply losing my mind. The walls are closing in on me. All the breath in my body the size of a small bird. But how can that bird take flight when there is no air to propel its weight, to make its heart soar?

I'm folding the minutes, the hours. I'm folding them into atoms of compressed, graspable comprehension. I can't manage anything beyond this. I imagine my mum is here folding time with me, like we used to at home, as easy as doing the bedsheets together. Bringing the ends back together with our fingertips, making the sheet flatter, thinner. Folding time. Making it smaller. *You take one end, I'll take the other.* Change time into something else. Concentrate and stay calm. *Please, Mum,* I say, *do it with me.* Keep folding. Here's a stray peg. Here's another. Run your fingers along the creases. That's it… Keep going. *Look, an origami swan!*

The house has already been turned inside out so many times before, because it's also where I work across multiple jobs, freelancing, employed, part-time, alongside all the work of care, phonics with my youngest child, boiling rice in a flat-bottomed pan, toast for breakfast, toast for dinner, licking the peanut butter spoon, wiping blood from a pillow when my youngest son has had a nosebleed. Where is the space for me now not to work in my own home? Where does the labour end and where does it begin?

I nearly birthed our first son on the bed I sit on, the spot where I usually teach. I sent myself into a trance-like state without drugs for two hours before they rushed me to the hospital. Now, another trance begins. Like the Princess in 'The Princess and the Pea', I can't stop thinking about the tiny specks of blood from the labour, little bloody dots or clots in time, buried deep within the layers of my mattress-mind.

Where does labour end?

Which bit of the day is my own and how do I know it belongs to me?

Me: licking the back of the peanut butter spoon.

Me: closing my eyes and enjoying the sun on my face as I open the door to the porch and take the recycling out to the bins near our garden gate.

Me: brushing the knots out of my hair and then pulling the stray strands out of the brush and disposing of them out of the bathroom window.

Online interviews erode the feeling of being comfortable in the place you're supposed to feel free and protected. My home is no longer a shelter, because I've ordered in the chaos plus dough balls. (I'm certainly not ordering in anything else because, unlike the rest of the universe, no one delivers take-aways to my rural postcode.) Somehow, I've to go on living and stake the chaos to the ground, trap it so I can let it go later. Maybe I can swallow it and contain it inside my own body. I have to take myself out of myself and shake the room out, too. Suspend it. Suspend myself, because I don't want it to take root in my heart. It's the feeling of falling. It's the feeling of failing. Failing, falling hard and your children's faces the instant you walk downstairs and they ask you how it went and you say you don't know.

I make a joke. I pop the kettle on. Sod it. It's not like I'm going down the mines.

A greenfinch or sparrow gets trapped in the porch. The birds make nests in the guttering directly above the entrance to our house, but as they come and go, I suspect, some of them end up flying straight through a sliding panel of glass in the porch, which we can't entirely close. Sometimes, they hit the glass and end up dazed on the tiled entrance. I cup the birds in my hands. How many winters will we have left in this house, which is now also the place where things fall out of the sky and we all hold on to them and pass them around? My hands holding the birds. My hands on the keys of my laptop. My hands carrying my children to bed. You win some, you lose some.

I'm mostly interviewed for fixed-term jobs, so even if I do succeed I know I'm no sooner in than back out of the door again. Like the poor birds in my porch, I'm also flying straight towards something hard, the window which isn't a window, the job which isn't really a job, each time smashing myself against the glass. Back downstairs, the birds keep coming in. It's hard not to think someone is sending me these birds as a warning. Then again, why should I be worried? It's not like I'm going down the mines. Or am I? Even I know that they once sent canaries down the mines to test the levels of oxygen before miners entered the pits. How is my breathing, right now? I don't know. How about yours?

A few years ago, at a child's birthday party, we arrived early and I thought it would be fun to answer the door for them. I bounded towards the hallway like an excitable, black-haired Labrador, and when the other visitors arrived I pretended the family living in the house had moved. I closed the door and giggled back down the hallway, impressed with my own dead-pan performance, before sending my friends back to the door, apologising on my behalf. Now, no one ever visits, except the others, who send chills through the house even though all the windows are closed and the air is a thick, hanging gauze, which makes a mausoleum of every damn, once-habitable space. Even the airing cupboard is a sad enclosure, full of things I never wear anymore, greying socks that haven't seen the light of day, towels no longer in use, because just the one is good enough for all of us, now that our bodies rarely even graze against the outer edges of the outside world.

I closed the blinds in my bedroom, piled my laptop on to a small plastic storage container and brought a chair into the room. I turned on a lamp and got a glass of water. Ritual aesthetic, though it never felt like that at the beginning, because I had hoped a job would happen. My children were often in the house. My dog was often in the house. I could hear my children bickering. Eventually, I heard the sound of *Minecraft* being played.

The door to the living room closes downstairs. I click on the link. Sometimes, the link doesn't work. I try again. Ouija board adventures. *Hello? Hello?* I have a moment to judge whether or not they know who I am, because it's a very small world. If they don't know me, I can be reborn again. I can be anyone. It's me on the board. My body is being pulled over there, but my mind hasn't caught up with it yet. Or, perhaps it's the other way around. I don't know. Does it matter?

Now, move along the letters on the board. Whooooosh. Push the pointer. Is it me moving, or is it just the wind? Someone speaks, but I'm tumbling through portals. Which door to go through? Should I pretend to be someone else? No, better not try that again.

In their individual rooms, on the other side, I can feel myself moving along the Ouija board and into the air. The interviewers are tuning in, I am tuning in. I switch on my microphone and I test it. A beat. Smiling faces, some more smiley than others. That Microsoft Outlook sound effect when you receive an email and then their eyes looking over at their emails while I am talking. The sound of a few audible clicks – impolite, I think, but nevertheless I have to accept this, as I accept the general apathy.

Aside from the email sound effects, which they just don't turn off for some reason, the process has a sleek form and style. It must stick to this. It has its own banal rhythm. By the time someone speaks, after introductions, statements, the testing of technology and announcements – *We're joined by someone you weren't expecting, we're sorry about this, but...–* finally, the questions arrive and I'm already dazed, because jumping through portals is so very tiring. Strangely, the questions are nearly always the same. In no particular order, I am asked multiple versions of these questions:

> *Explain your understanding of equality, diversity and inclusion issues.*
> *How they may impact on academic content and issues relating to student need.*
> *How do you contribute towards quality assurance?*

Explain your ability to develop familiarity with a variety
of strategies to promote and assess learning/information.
How is your work world leading?

I had once hoped for the kind of good old-fashioned interview style, where people asked specific questions about my work, in a positive way, teasing out the nuances of a certain role or questioning how I would develop new ideas, new work. But this is a lie I have told myself. With the often suffocating pressures of HR policies and procedures, best practice initiatives, not to mention the institutional 'biting-down' hard on what they call their commitment to equality, diversity and inclusion, interviews have become an endurance test.

Inevitably, the tick-boxing strategy of EDI policies, the insistent rolling out of objectives and newly aligned standards, means I have sometimes been interviewed for jobs because I have literally *ticked a box*. I know this, because the panel's eyes are glazed over and it's clear they aren't listening to me, even if they have invited me into this situation. Other times, it's a combination of being able to tick that box, being outstanding, but also being over-skilled, too 'good', meaning they won't want to pay more, or my profile won't fit the certain dynamic they want. They already have senior people draining them at the top end of the pay scale. I know this, because people speak differently outside of the system and send messages of support to me via their private email or social media. I love every single one of those people who did that. I'm thanking you all now (I'm sending you a 'folded hands in gratitude' emoji). Imagine if I didn't know? It's a mixed blessing, because some of those departments have since closed or made academics redundant.

We do that British thing where we talk about the weather. Really, that makes it worse because none of us are experiencing the same weather at all. That's the point, I suppose: we are all looking out at different parts of the same sky. I wish I could conjure myself into a storm, but they've trapped me in a bell jar.

They know they've got a good one here. There aren't many people like me doing interviews after a seventeen-year career, so they tend to want to see me. HR will give me an interview because I'm ticking all the boxes. I'm outstanding, I've embodied their wish list, but that means I'm also a problem, because they need to employ the cheaper ones, the younger ones, the ones they already know. It is always, I regret, the ones they already know. If they don't know them, it's the preppy guy with the chinos – you know the drill. I've been around a long time, so I'm often one of those people they have already heard of, or know on the scene, but still they go for another white male, because the system knows that; it recognises that subject position as the 'origin' data, the master key. I'm disrupting the process, because it hasn't thought about me. I'm an anomaly. What kind of game is this? They treat me like the Jeff Bridges character in *Tron*, a hacker uploading into the mainframe. Hieroglyph-ghost in the machine.

In this system, I couldn't get a job that was fractional and fixed-term, the lowest rung on the ladder. Yet, I gobbled up the opportunities, forgetting that I was eating out of the garbage bin. After my contract ended with The Tower university, they had me back for several interviews like a little whip they couldn't stop cracking, flinging it up into the air, faster, quicker, more furiously, even after I had finished working for them. I left, but they made me work the interview rounds while my children ate toast on the sofa and their whips cracked, and my body cracked, and then it was burned all over again by the whooping sound above my head, and I felt compelled to say *sorry, sorry*, because I must had done something wrong – *sorry I'm so useless, sorry, sorry*. My failed job interviews became a way of apologising and being branded as a failure even after my contract had ended.

I carried on cowering in the dark. I couldn't get a short-term contract for one day a week for six months. Two days a week for twelve months. One day a week for two years. One day a week for one year. Academia ate itself, bargained with itself, as I grew smaller and smaller.

I'm going to go through this carefully now, so you can see the cracks, the little fault lines, before you see me at their centre.

There are usually four people on screen. Up close, you can see their every flinch. The cameras capture their shame, if they have any, as they avoid giving you the job. I know all of the looks. Most of the time they know who they'll give the job to, so there's the 'visibly bored' look, the 'disappointed' look because they really wanted you, and the 'it's never going to happen' look, polite but vacant. Or they just go through the motions, nodding, nodding, looking down, looking sideways. Thinking about lunch. They read out their questions from prompts. Someone's dog barks off-screen. Sometimes, the dog is mine.

We carry on and I give a presentation. Two minutes... five minutes. I have a list of prompts next to the laptop, so I'm super able to articulate all my points within the timings. Please note that the tone of some of the panel can be a little aggressive, because they are more junior than me, but I'm applying for a junior role – there simply aren't any senior jobs. I backtrack and tell them I'm still on a journey, still learning and I've learned a lot during the pandemic. They go quiet. They don't want to hear that.

No one ever really talks about money, except for one professor who asks what I would want to be paid. I carefully try to avoid asking for the lowest amount, maybe somewhere in the middle, but I still don't get that job. Something makes me think that I should have put a number on it, I should have asked for the lowest amount. I try to work out how to pay our bills on a lower income and I realise I won't be able to afford to give up my Saturday job prepping kids for their A levels. I kind of like that Saturday job anyway. My expectations shrink and expand like a magic bath toy.

In some alternate reality, which I was too naive to know about back then, the people who are being offered the jobs are taking at least eight weeks to decide whether or not to sign the contract, playing hardball with HR and their employer, using the job offer to secure a promotion or a higher rate of pay in their current job. If that doesn't work, they play hardball again and hold out for more money or better terms. They even ask to change the job title. Another month might pass, but it has to be done. Such slick operations. I'm almost in awe of these bandits, but then I know it's not right. I don't ever want to feel like I'm playing poker with our lives.

I only ever go for two types of job: teaching and research, where you teach and you write stuff. You get maybe one day a week to write academic papers, or apply for grants, and if you're lucky you get to apply for a limited budget for travel to conferences around the world. Then there's teaching only, which means all your hours are dedicated to teaching and administration. The permanent people go here and there, here and there, here and there, travel, roaming, which, from the outside, looks a bit like they are on some kind of perpetual grand tour. My father had a particular word for roaming – *loafing*.

To loaf: idle, loaf, lounge, loll, laze, meaning to spend time doing nothing. To idle may be used in reference to persons that move lazily or without purpose, e.g. 'idled the day away'.

This is a problem for me because I've been a 'loafer', too. I'm a bit ashamed of that, even though I know it's more complex than it sounds; it confuses labour with pleasure and, worse still, at least in the way my father used it, it implies a feckless amount of leisure and tourism. This misconception doesn't account for the multiple modes of labour you have to participate in as a result of that activity taking you to other, similarly well-appointed campuses within striking distance of coffee shops and museums which you might skirt around, but never experience in any meaningful way because you're still at work. You have your work face on, doing work-facing things. You are labouring and it can be very productive, exciting, inspirational. But that feeling of shame persists. That shame is intricately bound up with my sense of class, gender, ethnicity. If I were a white male in beige chinos, I would feel no shame. In fact, I would be very much like a *flâneur*:

> Flâneur: an idle stroller who is in their element as one of the crowd. A passionate observer who is at the centre of his world and yet remains inconspicuous. (Charles Baudelaire)

'Loafing' is about avoiding the mechanisms of capitalism, production and labour; it's actually a really good way to describe the use of time that simply avoids work altogether. You could, in theory, *loaf off* in your mind while sat at your desk at work. The thing is – the thing I know – is that you can't 'loaf' off to an academic conference, but because my dad didn't understand these more privileged forms of employment usually reserved for the middle classes, he went on using the word 'loafing' to describe the work I undertook outside of campus. On the other hand, it was all right for him to 'loaf' down the bookies all the time, or down the 'office', as he called it.

Even after he's long gone, I go around with the word 'loafer' in my head, arguing with my dad's ghost as I sit on the train. He gets comfortable in the seat next to me and unfolds a copy of the *Daily Mirror* with the racing section at the back. He grimaces, but says nothing, his lips pursing, tension around his jawline. He clears his throat and turns a page of the newspaper. I know he always wins the argument even before he tells me, or rather the page he's staring at. He tells me I don't know how to graft. He's a bit hard on me. I buy another black coffee in a polystyrene cup and look out of the window. He lifts his head from the newspaper and tells me the coffee is very over-priced. While he's at it, criticising my job choices, he reminds me not to burn my tongue on the coffee.

I wonder about my father's views on labour. When I was small, I used to go to his office in Staines and pretend I was his secretary, playing with the photocopier while he checked in on the factory workers in the warehouse and collected payslips in brown envelopes. I used to love pressing all the buttons and watching the paper fly out, warm as toast. His real secretary was called Shushma and she always had a hardboiled sweet on her desk for me and a warm compliment about my hair or my patent-leather shoes. In the grounds outside, there were large white mushrooms the size of footballs, which I instinctively kicked into the grass. Playgrounds, they come in all shapes and sizes.

My father never expected me to earn lots of money or to be successful in the way I overheard other parents speak to their children at parents' evenings or at the supermarket, reminding them how much things cost and how you have to better yourself to do well in this life. I don't recall him ever wishing that for me, which is odd now I come to think of it. What kind of parent does that? One that was a prisoner of war, perhaps. One whose ideas about the material world were shaped by an early childhood spent in a monastery and later years watching all that was solid smash into the air as war descended upon his homeland. He just wanted me to be happy. I can't recall him ever telling me to get a really good job, though he must have wished for me every success. He praised my cooking, the way I learned from him how to mask off areas with tape when decorating a room, the way I seemed to get on with things on my own, as he would have done, using my own initiative. He rarely congratulated me on my academic achievements. The kind of success I achieved was something he didn't really understand. He didn't care about French philosophy or feminist art. It was *my* success, mine alone, and I suppose that's a bit sad. Admittedly, I think he was glad I was interested in something.

Am I happy now? my dad asks me on the train. *Can we come back to that question later, please, Dad? Look, I say, look, we're going past Vauxhall Bridge now. Look, look how tall the build-ings are.* I try to remember what happiness felt like, kicking mushrooms as big as footballs.

Precariously employed people like me will leave after a year and no one will really notice. HR will request their laptop back and the system will lock you out on the last day of your contract. An anonymous person will walk over to the main reception desk and smile as they take back any property of theirs and you will be friendly, because, after all, they're only doing their job. Sometimes, like a little latchkey kid, I could return via things like associate fellowships, which meant I could still access my email, borrow books from the library, but not be paid. These fellowships also have to be authorised, because they cost the institutions money, so it's not an expectation at all, yet you need to continue to use the library in order to keep a foot in the world you wish to belong to. Permanent jobs have 'research hours'. There are also research-*only* jobs, but these are often for a fixed period of time. So many ways to fall. What happens to people on a part-time contract for a fixed-term period? What happens to others interviewed for those jobs, the ones like me who were left behind? I wasn't even being force-fed crumbs, because they would take the food out of my mouth as soon as it left their fingers. *Have you finished with that?*

There are some advantages to being interviewed online. It means you can surreptitiously glance down at a notepad and keep track of all the major winning points you wanted to get in. You can listen out for the postman and disappear if you really have to, though that never happens. You can, in theory, wear anything you like on your lower half, like jogging bottoms, but I never did, because I was already doing the interviews in my bedroom and that's enough for me. I did a really good job of pretending I wasn't at home. I made *them* feel at home. I'm generous like that. My children didn't make a sound and the doorbell never rang; nor did I cry nor show any signs of anger or disappointment, tiredness or frustration, especially when they asked me back for another round of interviews for the same job. I was such a good girl. I swallowed my fury. I sipped water and tied jade beads around my ancestors' necks, asking them to be quiet just one more time, please, because I needed money. My hieroglyph bones made, I'll admit, a lovely yawning noise as they shifted into their old enslaved ways, because, after all, it felt like home.

After I'd exhausted all the possible career opportunities within my particular discipline, I started to apply for a whole range of roles across the arts sector. The world opened up to me and I started to see a life beyond the one I had led for so long. I could do this. I could *become*. But the interview questions were very similar. I became quite good at preparing in advance, because I knew what they would ask me. Stupidly, I hoped and dreamed, while I was hit with something hard. I went back into the interview scenario, over and over, as if I had amnesia. That reminds me, what's that syndrome called where you keep exposing yourself to damaging environments? I suppose it doesn't matter what it's called, because I need to work and my children eat a lot of food which I have to buy, regularly. There's no time to overthink this. I just have to go again. So here I go. Deep breath.

Can you provide an example of when you were most effective and problem-solved a complex situation?

Complex situation… Very quickly, I started to think of myself as Sonic from *Sonic the Hedgehog*, speeding through so many interviews and dying at the end of every single one of them. Arms outstretched, dropping down. I could hear that awful 'bong' noise, which was so effective and gutting in the videogame. I constructed perfect answers for each question and over time I learned how to perform, visibly, the process of affected thoughtfulness, which is ironic given the field I was applying within. I paused. I looked away from the screen.

Feedback told me to be more 'thoughtful', to take more time, but this didn't matter, because I still didn't get any jobs. HR demands something useful be said, but because they couldn't fault me, they lied. They suggested I work on developing my research (four pages long on my CV), because I had done too much teaching; too much research and not experienced enough as a teacher; too long, too short, too this, too that. I tried not to laugh as they told me I was really, 'really' good, but didn't have enough experience, or I didn't give enough information in the interview. People try to shuffle themselves out of responsibility.

They said I should think about my 'brand'. To hear such a statement levelled at me from someone in a position of seniority reminds me of how academia is just another brand I've been buying all of my life and its various institutional settings were merely consumer choices plus fries. It's hard not to think about the argument Naomi Klein makes in her book *No Logo*. She explains why multinational corporations, historically targeted at the youth market, privilege the manufacturing of their brand over the actual manufacturing of the goods themselves. I always thought it was funny how the interview questions rarely go into any detail about my work experience or career history. This, I suspect, is because they simply require the basic operations, the manufacturing skills, the labour that will correctly support their brand. I tried to tell them I was a human being, but all they wanted was my pledge to their brand and for me to write books and give lectures that conformed to their marketing strategy.

I wondered what the logo for this certain situation would look like. It was already on my lips before I had thought about it. I imagined it was the word 'possession' with the first 'o' floating above the rest of the word like a faceless head or the mouth of a tunnel, a passage. My brand was my ancestors splitting chicken heads from their bodies before they boiled them in a pot; my brand was brass coils and listening to Tina Turner in a cave; peanut butter licked off a spoon; Salome and Medusa; oakmoss and dandelions; the wind, the wind; starlings nested inside an aproned woman's pocket.

Sometimes I didn't want to hear the voices again, but I heard them anyway. They would not leave. Even on this side of the Ouija board, you can hear their voices penetrating the thresholds of other worlds. Many knew I really needed a job but, still, I heard the noise of the deathly *Bong – time's up, you're dead!* Sonic used to drop down and exit the screen in a weird, bungee-jumping kind of movement when he died, as if he were being pushed out of the world of the game. He didn't even die *in* the game. Why was that?

Booong! Leave this plane of reality, go away, you lost! Bong!

I collected so many golden rings, hit so many targets with my answers – whoooosshhh – but still the game was too difficult. Damn that bloody game. I wanted the golden rings, but all I ever got were the swinging obstacles hitting me in the face. If you go on YouTube, you can watch a completed version of the original Sega Mega Drive *Sonic the Hedgehog* game. The video lasts around forty-five minutes. That's the average length of a job interview.

Explain your ability to develop familiarity with a variety of strategies to promote and assess the sharing of information.

I like this question. This question is really asking a lot of BIG things, but mainly it is just asking how you will be, and how you will always be, a multi-tasking genie in a bottle.

How do you teach online, in person, both at the same time, via online systems, the marking systems, the various interfaces/ Zoom/Microsoft Teams/using slides, using your voice, using recordings of your voice, using videos of yourself, using links to other people's videos/ talking without using a camera, talking while being transcribed for the subtitled version…?

I get very bored somewhere between the interviews I've done in 2020 and the ones in 2022. I start answering these questions a little more truthfully. I start answering most questions like this, because it's the only way. I tell them about how we are still learning and we won't know how this has worked, or how effective online teaching really is, for many years, years from now. We won't really know if all these new models of learning have been truly useful. I hope they have been. But the institutions don't want to hear any of this. This means that they might not be able to enter a global market. It means they might die. I die, so they won't have to. My face, then, a *memento mori*.

Oh God, I tried so hard not to do that. I make myself so obedient and good, so professional. I endeavour to be virtuous, but what's the point when I know they've got the scythes out, ready to decapitate me in some cornfield, like Saint Sidwella.

Bong!

After thirty interviews over a few years, it finally dawns on me. I know I'm probably the only person the panel has seen all day whose answers resonate with compassion and truth. I can't see any point in not telling the truth. It's a moment when they need to listen. I throw the whole damn thing at them. I tick all the boxes and then I give them well-phrased, philosophical answers.

Then, in a moment of panic, I try to grab the jade around my neck. I ask my ancestors to love me. I need their love because I'm scared and I can't go on dying and dying and dying.

I was in my very own performance art, just like Marina. Even if I could cry, as I watched all those potential jobs hit the bottom of a river, or the data stream, I felt nothing. Paralysis is a consequence of possession.

Explain your understanding of equality, diversity and inclusion issues.

Breathe. The right answer could be:

I believe in the values of _____. I support and value _____ I have received training and attend regular workshops in order to ensure I meet the needs of the institution and I believe education should be inclusive and materials should support different learning styles. We should support diversity and equality in teaching and I actively do this as a role model.

Breathe. But this is not the answer I want to give. This is not what I want to say. It's likely I will be the only woman of colour interviewed with a CV like mine, with caring responsibilities and in a precarious position. I weigh this up. *So, I've been thinking,* I say, *I feel it's important for me to say a few things.* It's my own way of protecting myself. Yet the process continues without delay. Someone in HR says I'm really good at speaking from the perspective of lived experience. I should be a consultant for that (thanks!). How do I become a consultant and how much does it pay? Which version of me do they want? I keep thinking about the many files on my laptop of cover letters for jobs and versions of my CV. These files clog up my documents folder, alongside P45s, invoices and tax returns. I try to answer every question evenly, calmly, but perhaps I've said too much this time. Perhaps I should stop telling them what I actually think. After all, I'm not here to put ideas into their heads; that's the last thing any academic in this century should do.

Bong!

At the end of every interview, I turn off the laptop, pull back the curtains in my bedroom and move the little chair I usually use to give the impression I'm at a desk. I like to ensure they get a view of my mantelpiece stacked with books. It mirrors what I often see on-screen when they talk, so I reckon this makes them feel assured that I'm just like them. But I take things off. After every interview, I put things back on again. I see myself on the screen. I study my movements and my voice as I talk and adjust them in real time. That's just it, isn't it? All job interviews seem to take place online now, originally out of necessity during the pandemic, but I still can't really fathom why this has become the 'new normal'. I strongly suspect it's deliberate: it's important they get the online version of me, because what they are really doing is interviewing an optional mode of 'me' that their institution will approve of and interact with largely online. It's a rehearsal, a screen test, a casting couch.

My friend Malika is laughing again. She tells me my fate is coming. I'll never get another job. My ancestors aren't interested in any of this. *Quick, quick,* they say, the sun has come out and I should go and pick snowdrops near the river. They are so funny, like excited children. They tell me they have grown to love England, looking out at the world from inside my hieroglyph bones. They erase the bitterness with a single gesture of love. A single breath. A snowdrop flowering on the verge. I know I need to get to that place near the verge – I need to turn the handle to the bedroom door, put my shoes on, collect the mail that has fallen on to the doormat – but when I close my eyes they are still filled with the blue light from my screen. I can't move. It's like a siren song, that light.

Before I go, I check I've turned off the plug to my laptop. I don't want a fire. The room is so still. Shadows passing over the folds on the bedsheet. The imprint where the laptop once sat on the bed, on top of a plastic storage box, which holds my son's favourite toy cars. Books on my shelves, leaning in all directions, balancing on each other, waiting for a hand to prop them up again. (I'm also waiting for a hand, any hand, to prop me up again.) On the mantel, I return a pink Mother's Day card to its original position facing outwards, towards where I usually sit on the bed. The card was made at school by my eldest son, a paper cut-out of his photographed face blowing a kiss from deep within his palm. A trail of heart-shaped cut-outs scatter towards the edges of the card. My son is wearing his school uniform and his hair is more of a mullet than it usually is, because the card was made at some point during the second year of the pandemic and we couldn't work out which hairdressers were open and which had taken a hiatus and furloughed their staff.

Before the interview, I had moved the card, because I feared it was my motherhood that might have been preventing me from getting a job. What if they think I won't perform as well because I have small kids? Do I really think that? I wonder. Either way, I don't want to remind them that I have… a life. I'll do anything now. I just need to roll the right dice. Hit the right notes. Sing the right song. Won't someone tell me how to do this? Why don't I know? Why can't I do it? I look at the card and then I look at the place where the laptop had been. I vow to never move my son's card again. If they don't like it, they can lump it. I tried to banish him, even him, as I tried to banish my wobbly-headed ancestors. I cherish his little cut-out head. I love him. He cut out those hearts for me. In return, I'll go on cutting mine out for him, again and again and again. *Snip, snip, snip.*

Then, a child calls out for something. *I'm coming, Mummy's coming.*

When I wasn't being interviewed, I began to write a story about the ones I had lost. Writing them back into existence made me feel like I existed, too. I missed my family, I longed for their presence – my father, my aunt, my two grandmothers, my mother as well, because she had late-stage dementia and her mind was almost gone (I cared for her on the days when I wasn't with the children or teaching, but that's another story).

In the small hours, unable to sleep, I began to sense my elderly aunt was standing amongst the barley, in her usual cloud of Samsara perfume, and she was watching me, waiting for me to turn towards her. At first, I avoided her gaze. I kept my head down, because I didn't want her to judge me. Nevertheless, there she was, and my father as well, sometimes smoking an Old Holborn roll-up with his cricket hat on. He was facing away from me, looking out to the pink rendered walls of the old thatched cottage on the corner, or the towering pylons, which draped themselves across an old, crumbling bridge. I had never seen my family anywhere near this kind of English pastoral 'scene' – they lived in London all of their lives (apart from when they lived in India and Burma)

– yet there they were and I accepted them. All these years, I had forgotten them in the search for work and the endless chaos of having small children. Adrift, my family ghosts got tethered to the fields. A snatch of yellowing wool pinned by a gust of air to a wire fence.

I made something – a storm-wracked, ship-shaped book, which carried all my family safe inside. They'll always be there now. For them, I turned the world sideways and the sun and the moon retreated. I carried them close.

It's the end of the day. It's getting dark outside and I'm feeling very tired. I think I've got a cold coming on. Something doesn't feel right. If you play with a Ouija board too many times, you disturb the others. I can hear breathing inside the walls, down the chimney breast. Maybe it's time I left the board and folded it away. I should put it away forever. I could bury it in the garden, but I can't quite bring myself to do this. Not yet.

At night, I still worry I'm being possessed.

I take the silver scissors from the kitchen drawer and cut all of the plugs loose from their cables, severing them from their tails. Another. And another. I have the scissors in my hands and I'm jabbing at all the wires. It's not enough, so I go to the porch and seek out the mains electricity box and switch off all of the power. The house is plunged into darkness.

I can hear myself breathing. I try to meditate while I hold on to the scissors shining in the tiniest trickle of light from the moon outside. Decapitated plugs in my lap like seed heads waiting to be sown under the spectre of a harvest moon. Their solid weight in my lap.

9

The Buds of a Sycamore Tree

Inside the museum, behind a big black curtain is the sun suspended in a room. Red and green giant beanbags still hold the slumped shapes of small visitors who gazed at the molten core, transfixed by its golden lullaby. My youngest son is now a satellite, like the Hinode exploring a magnetic field, or the Parker Solo Probe. He makes a silhouette, he makes a sound. Solar wind becomes his breath. Radio waves transmit his nervous energy into beams of light on his cheeks, across the back of his arms. The tiny hairs on the back of his neck are aglow in the synthetic drama of a giant star turning, turning slowly and catching on fire.

Questions, so many questions, interrupt the slow cinema of the sun's wavelengths. We are running around at a museum in Swindon and for the first time in many years I'm able to watch my children watch the world without interruption or the fear of failing, the fear of falling. My hieroglyph bones are too tired to spring into action, but that doesn't matter, because I'm swept up in the movement of my children who spin around me. I pick them up, pointing out things in the dark. I find myself looking at them without thinking of so many other things at the same time. I have waited too long for this. A sly, solemn feeling. I love them. Just for a moment, I can see them and only them. I have turned off my computer and my phone is on silent.

It's half term and I'm not breaking into a sweat when they enter the gift shop. We walk out with a pencil sharpener shaped like a rocket and a set of glow-in-the-dark planets. I take them to the café and I buy two large sausage rolls, a Diet Coke, a chocolate brownie, a medium-sized chocolate chip cookie and a regular cup of coffee. I've spent £25 and I'm still twirling around the museum, under all the flickering lights, as buttons are pressed and things are observed from above or below. We stand inside a replica of a space shuttle and we press more buttons and listen to pre-recorded sound effects of jets and blasts, all the razzle and all the dazzle. Why can't all our days be like this? The museum swallows my £25 and I eat the joy of just giving them what they want. People say it's wrong to give your children what they want, don't they? Well, what if... what if there's this one moment where what they want is exactly what they need and it's what you need, too.

If I give you £25, or a little piece of my body and my breath, my thoughts in the night, my hope, what's left of my dreams, will you give me what I want for five minutes? Five minutes. Start the clock. I've packed it all up in a bag for life for you. I've even handed you a receipt (this is the receipt). Don't look in the bag yet, because you might be a bit disappointed, but it's all I have left. There are still some good bits, which you shouldn't waste. Down there, that's my soul ground from multiple origin beans, wit distilled from years of bearing witness and not being crushed, determination carefully crafted from ethically sourced grains of resilience. That £25 buys you quite a bundle of my thoughts and ideas, because it's hard to trade them, in these times, so here they are. They light up the bag like glow sticks in purple, orange and blue. Take one for yourself, I'm OK with that. Keep it. Here, have another. I'll give you this and you give me five minutes of what I want.

Hold on to that five minutes and put the music on. I'll dance to anything, just give me a beat. When I was alone and my children wouldn't sleep, I always put some music on and danced with them on my hips, strapped to me in a baby carrier. When my first son was born in 2012, the British girl band Little Mix, the ones that look like they've formed a band at the end of their shift in Superdrug, were number one in the charts with their song 'Wings'. These girls reminded me so much of the girl gang I once knew back home in Hayes and it was *their* voices that I heard singing back to me then, telling me to fly.

I had last seen some of my old gang around the time of my twenty-first birthday. I wore a red *lehenga* (skirt and fitted top) and Malika had brought a bottle of Lambrini. Forgotten for almost a decade, their faces appeared by the cot. I rocked my son to sleep and wondered where my friends had gone. I was all alone in my weird, bittersweet connection to music, which took me back to a different kind of home. I had defied the Fates, but what did that really count for if no one was witness to that except me? I missed them, I missed the part of myself that had once tied her shirt around her waist and drawn a brown line around her lips, filling it in with lip gloss. The girl who danced with her gang and did a group performance in front of the whole school to R. Kelly's 'She's Got That Vibe'.

Rhythms make a life, make a living. I continued to dance with my children throughout their infancy and now one of them is almost a teenager and making up his own moves.

We have a set list of music we play on a loop, alongside the radio when all the devices have run out of battery. I cook the dinner while we switch from heavy metal to UK garage music or punk, Queen, the Rolling Stones, Madonna or Nina Simone. There is clapping and intermittent wiggling of our hips. Singing out of tune and humming to the beats when we don't know the words. Out of breath, we stop and laugh. *I used to listen to that when I was your age*, I say. They listen to everything. They know how to dance. We're dancing to Kiss FM and Magic FM and even Radio 2. We are flipping on to our backs and free-styling, doing our dodgy dance moves in the kitchen. Someone is turning the volume dial up and down. One child is dancing around the table, circling it like a hobbling goblin, while the other is breakdancing like a crab on its back because he saw that somewhere on YouTube. The dog is barking and we are moving. The whole place is rocking.

For a long time, I had stopped dancing with them in the kitchen, but now the feeling has returned. I hope we won't stop dancing together. At the moment, it's often 'Treat People with Kindness' by Harry Styles, which my eldest son has a fondness for precisely because his deputy headmaster often uses it as a warm-up before he starts his assemblies. We do a flapper-style jive in the room, just like they do in the video. No one is watching. We don't care.

All of us avoid the homework. I'll have to admit that the way my children are taught to learn at school makes my heart sink. I understand they have to acquire the basic facts, but there's no room for genuine creativity, freedom to think, to move around the ideas. I want to try to share what I know, but it seems so far removed, so abstract. My academic background and career in Higher Education affords me the ability to see all the way to the end, or to the very 'top of the tree', but this is somewhat of a curse when it comes to opening up my children's homework books. I have to climb back down the tree in order to gain some common ground with my children. I have to go backwards, but that's hard because I can't make sense of it all. I worry, because they face daily exposure to a world stifled by the system's almost obscene faith in 'learning by rote'. The rebel in me wants to subvert things a little, to go off grid. I challenge them with a bit of French cinema or metaphysical poems about tigers and jaguars. Like those beasts, I want them to be wild, to let their souls remain open to the world. I want to stand in the way of them being tamed by an education system that is, frankly, letting them down. For a moment, I try to set them free.

As for home-schooling, it's not an option because I have to work and, as the pandemic has taught us all, teaching small children requires a certain amount of lion-heartedness and the patience of a saint, both of which are qualities I'm still praying for. Perhaps in the next life I'll do better.

Christ almighty, it's 2022 and I've just been given a full-time, fixed-term contract at a Russell Group university. Lucky job interview no. 31. A year of full-time wages, another year of mortgage payments and food bills, repairs on the house, insurances, car repayments, fuel bills and council tax. A year of new possibilities and another ID card flung around my neck. A year of something that I don't have to leave for a while. I'm so tired that I take this job as a holiday from the job interviews, which, if I'm not asked to stay on, will have to start again soon.

For years now, I've thought about what it would be like to get a full-time, permanent job and all the things I would do to celebrate. This mainly involves going to a five-star hotel and ordering afternoon tea in a room upholstered wall to wall in thick, thick carpets and paisley prints; going to Liberty and buying myself an exquisite gold ring with tiny sapphires set into it as if they were stars (because I've looked at it many times and social media accounts notice this, so they keep sending me the same image until I'm obsessed); going to London and seeing friends I've not been able to afford to see for a while because of the expensive train ticket; buying a new jumper (100 per cent Scottish wool); buying new shoes, ordering the blinds for my second child's bedroom, which we got priced up a year after the pandemic. It's a pathetic list, I know.

In the absence of any permanent employment, I find myself in a science museum in Swindon with the kids, sharing a sausage roll after standing in the car park in the rain for ten minutes, looking for the ticket machine and then failing to download the parking app. I don't mind the rain. I'm just relieved about the fact that I've found some full-time work. But my ancestors are wobbling their funny little heads again and listening to my heartbeat. They don't like the sausage roll, nor the Diet Coke. I think they might be saying that I seem to be relaxing, settling in, and that's dangerous. I'm not safe, they tell me. I can't just stand there in the car park when the end is not this. *The end is not this!* I gave them the moon in Swindon and still they asked for more. I showed them a giant 3D image of the sun and a sparkly piece of rock from a meteor, but they kept on warning me and spitting out the sausage roll. Bland, greasy pastry all over the floor and on their faces. My youngest son drains the last of the Coke from its can – a small win because he is usually banned from imbibing such toxic beverages.

My ancestors asked me for chilli sauce, pork ribs and egg noodles, but I walked right past those and then they resented me all day for that. They guzzled lemonade and when that was gone they asked for more. Between mouthfuls, they told me to wake up, W A K E   U P, because I needed to think about what I'd done and make a plan, get it right, do it better. I was not doing it better. I was leaving my mind and body behind and even five minutes was too long. They carried on until they were able to make some of the muscles in my face twitch and my eyes hurt and my cheeks palpitate as if I was about to burst. They pinched my face and poked me in the eye. They stopped only when we got to the flight simulator and then they went oddly silent, praying I would never go in that thing again.

Quietly, they ask me what a black hole is. I say nothing can come back from a black hole, it consumes matter and nothing will ever stop it. They misunderstand me and hear the word 'blackout'. I say no, no, 'black hole… h-o-l-e', and they say we must shut all the doors and hide under the beds, because that means the bombs are coming and I say no, no, they're not, they're really not (not here anyway), but they carry on, so in the end I just agree with them. Yeah, I say, that's what a black hole is. As we shuffle once more through the gift shop, they remind me again: it's only a year of work…

Who will buy the Tunnock's Teacakes, then, after that? I told them they should never have tried the teacakes and sugar is an addiction. They've gone wild for those marshmallow teacakes. Withdrawal makes them anxious. I throw a sugar cube at them and they catch it between their fingers in one perfect movement, like that moment when Barack Obama caught a fly during a live television interview.

After half term, which is also reading week, I visit the campus and collect a new computer, a microphone, earphones, a charger and a spare USB stick. I'm issued with an email address and a username. There's now a number '3' after my surname on the email address, correlating with the amount of times I've worked here before, in the past, pre-pandemic. The number also seems to imply that, yes, there are three of me, three versions 'out there' and now they are all back here, together. The 'Holy Trinity' of Me.

What if each of those versions could speak and what would they say? When my mother first arrived in England, she worked in many factories, including one which manu-factured the black boxes used to record data from aircrafts. Are these words, now, the ones I write here, a kind of black box, holding together all the information which led to multi-ple endings or intermissions? During the plague, my children were deprived of social engagement and were forced to dream through the conduit of flickering black boxes, whose interaction with various algorithms tracked their activity in real time as if they, too, were faulty aircrafts, no longer able to fly. Despite my mother's work on these machines, she never flew. She spent almost thirty years living under Heathrow's flight path yet remained entirely unacquainted with the inside of an aeroplane.

I 'ping' back to life on the campus intranet as my password and username allows me access once more to the online teaching materials, the library, the SharePoints, email, departmental handbooks, payroll, HR, staff services and training workshops. Coming back to 'life', I'll admit, it's lovely to see familiar faces and the landscaped campus looks expensively radiant. My name appears on a door outside an office and for the first time in my life, I have somewhere to work. I never had an office before at my old, part-time permanent job, because, apparently, there weren't enough rooms in the five-storey, 9,000-square-foot building.

At The Tower university, I shared an office on the second floor, but I was rarely there in person and when I was it wasn't very comfortable. The corner office was painted brilliant white and it was west-facing, so the sun came in through windows with no blinds, casually burning the back of my eyes. In a horror film, this would be an excellent chamber for the capture and incineration of vampires, exposing them to its killer flares of light, which radiated from wall to wall, penetrating the backs of their blood-sucking heads. Entering into that chamber was like having your mind wiped, which was not right at all, given the educational, mind-expanding purpose of the building. And it was the institution whose ways were almost certainly vampiric – in every context, I was merely a snack. At any rate, I could not agree more with the idea Karl Marx put forward in *Das Kapital*, in which capital is 'dead labour', living only by sucking living labour, consuming more and more in order to gain life from the dead labour of others. While the system ate me, I visited the canteen, marginally preferring the banal, cookie-cutter space of the student refectory to the white chamber. I marvelled at the sale of locally brewed organic beer and chic wine in cute little bottles, stored next to peanut butter protein bars and the greenest of apples, the shiniest packets of carbon-neutral crisps.

Someone generously told me about another study space for Staff Only. This space existed in one of the Grade 1 listed buildings where you had to use your swipe card to get in. My card wasn't working so I crept around outside, peering into the Victorian windows. While I failed to gain entry into the

Staff Only area of my dreams, I did manage to use my swipe card to enter the Geography Department and the Classics Department, having meaningful, though happenstance, conversations with a whole number of interesting academics. Freedom to move around means freedom to interact and to find people in the corridors, or with their doors ajar, and you could go in and say hello and share your news, or ask them how they were – things that told me I was human, after all. That thing happened again, where students waited outside a seminar room and we all waited to go in. At last, we were all in that together again and we greeted each other in ways that didn't really need words. We simply shared the same air and it was marvellous.

Now, I won't lie about this – my name on the door of an office space is a truly sublime feeling. I push the door open. You can hear the blackbirds gathering on the cherry trees. You can hear the groundsmen coppicing some of the hazel trees and loading logs onto the back of a pick-up truck. I plug in the computer and turn on an Anglepoise lamp. I shouldn't be getting too comfortable, it's only a twelve-month contract, but I have to take what I can, enjoy what I can, so I dust down the desk and open up the emails. There's even a kitchen across the hallway. A kitchen! A kitchen that wasn't my kitchen at home. Things which weren't mine, cups of all shapes and sizes and packets of tea – a mug with a small illustration of a whale; rare and unusual Chinese tea, likely gifted to some colleague from an international student. I could rummage through to my heart's content, like the greedy magpie I knew I was. In the corridor – a real, actual corridor – students lingered and talked to me, while birds did their thing on the ancient trees outside and blue skies dropped their pretty, blue light through large panes of double-glazed glass. Just above the roofline, between the spires of the cathedral and the hills stretching out towards the sea, was a golden ring shaped just like the sun.

Drunk on sugar and outdoor light, which they had sorely missed, my ancestors flung off their brass coils and rested their heavy, heavy heads on silken pillows, closing their eyes and curling into oval-shaped balls, which resembled the buds on the sycamore trees on campus. They fell into a deep slumber that lasted for many months. I missed their funny little heads, but I was also glad of having the time to myself. First, they dreamed of dipping their hands into the waters of the Irrawaddy Delta and catching giant river prawns; someone cuts off the heads of the prawns and removes their insides, before mixing them with salt and drying them out on the decks of a boat. My ancestors imagine falling through clouds and dancing on the rooftops of the tea houses near the golden pagodas, but the sky is the wrong colour, like a weird neon blue. The trees are different too. One of them looks like a Burmese nat, a tree spirit. Closer, it looks like someone they've seen before. They think it looks like me.

Are you her, they ask? *The one who belongs to us?*

The tree is covered in oakmoss and amber-coloured sap from willows and elders – English trees.

They take out an immaculately wrapped Tunnock's Teacake: an offering to the tree who was also, they believed, a great forest guardian.

ရိုက္ကၒခၖဝ္ိၣၥး

While my ancestors dreamed, I attended research seminars and symposiums. I used the photocopier and stood in the corridors at 8.30 a.m., carrying books and climbing the staircases, going the wrong way, then back down again. I did things like peer reviews, drop-ins, pop-ins, departmental meetings and taster sessions for school students in the local area. I sat and fought with a greedy seagull who tried to snatch the end of the baguette I was eating. I watched a whole orchestra come in and rehearse in one of the halls. Over time, I grew to love the campus as if it were a recently terraformed community on a distant planet. I saw the seedlings of new trees being planted and bodies of water flowed all around impressive buildings, which held every amenity imaginable. There was never any waste or litter visible. Everywhere, doors opened automatically. I thought I had finally stopped orbiting and I had arrived on this new planet, which was busy, so busy, and full of potential. Love and hope, just two things, to carry now in my body, lighter without my ancestors bopping their heads up and down, peering out of my hieroglyph bones. No longer did I sense their cloying presence, as if they were constantly pulling at my net curtains in order to catch a glimpse of the neighbours.

I found myself sifting through old school photographs discovered at the back of a cupboard. I decided to get back in touch with Malika and we arranged a phone call. We had remained friends on social media, but that was it. She told me excitedly over the phone how she had recently moved to Cambridgeshire with her two children, eighty miles north of our hometown. I told her I went further, a few hundred miles further away, southwest of Hayes.

After that conversation, I had the strongest urge to hold my first child and sing to him from a song I thought I had forgotten, a voice I had left far behind me. It rose from me, as easy as a knife passes through butter. I wrote it down, laughing as I adjusted to the beat.

THE BUDS OF A SYCAMORE TREE

Mother tongue, once in London town, all vowels long,
    and nice and sweet.
Accented, freshly cut into the words, foreign flavour, give
    me the subtitles please!
School vocabulary, flips American rap and R&B.
Words don't make sense like that, though I like the flow.
So I practise my other kind of therapy, English with a
    cup of tea, Radio 4 and Merchant Ivory.
A little of them and a little of me, eccentric with a
    capital 'E',
Code switching, incessantly, becomes normal, invariably,
    proper jokes,
this switching thing, adapting, but staying free, you and
    me, sat together comfortably.
Last time we were in Hayes getting checked in our garms,
going back to your yard for food your little brother
    made us.
Words, sweet and sour in our mouths, passing the time
    with our rhythms,
codes within codes, clothes, even swapping those (my
    trousers, because they looked better on your thighs).
Your schoolgirl fight, police sirens and saving face,
I cried when you left but now you got your own kids
and I never write.

After all these years, the seed of Malika's voice was still hard and silent inside of me as my children grew. Silted words gathered in our orchards.

Putting on my jetpack and leaving this offshore world, from time to time, I walked around the city. First, I paid my respects to Saint Sidwella's mural on the high street, then I went to the museum and I saw an ammonite, an elephant and a tiger. I climbed up a hill and looked out to the quayside, which led to a place where there was an orchard, canal boats and a pub with the smoke of a wood burner coming out of its chimney. I crossed an iron bridge and I walked past a row of Victorian cottages with different coloured doors and pots of tulips outside. I travelled past another avenue of houses and then I walked back towards the city and up another hill near the ruins of a castle. Here, I reached a spot which I had heard of before, but never visited.

At the ruins of the castle's gatehouse, there was a little silver plaque with an engraving neatly etched on to it with words that told me this was the place where the last four 'witches' in England were tried before they were hanged more than 300 years ago. You wouldn't notice the plaque if you were to pass by, but I stopped there for a while, my hands touching it, cold and smooth under my fingertips. Down the street, people were buying flat whites and queueing for the bus. Everyone knows that the four women had done nothing wrong. They were hanged from a tree that stood not far from here. How can that sentence be true? Read it again.

Temperance Lloyd, Mary Trembles, Susannah Edwards and Alice Molland, four women from Bideford, were accused of witchcraft and 'discoursing' with the devil. According to the accounts of witnesses at the trial, Lloyd confessed to turning herself into a black cat and 'fornicating' with a male figure, who also took the form of a magpie. The court heard how Trembles and Edwards had caused a woman to develop poor health, curiously, the same woman they had earlier begged food from in the street. During the trial, Edwards hexed a man, causing him to fit and shake uncontrollably on the floor. The memorial was erected 'In the hope of an end to persecution & intolerance'. As I read the words over and over, over and over, something loosened in my throat and at my neck. The strange, uncanny sensation of a rope unwinding. I remembered the woman dancing in the cave and the painting of the lamb, the murmuration of swifts and the Burmese cat. Sets of brass coils and jade necklaces, bowls of *hin* soup and hundreds of betel nuts shivering on the floor.

I looked at the plaque. I kept looking and I stayed very still. I listened to seagulls fly over my head. I could hear the wind lick the ancient bricks and loosen the tiniest fragments of grit and loam. Ants moved near the soil at my feet, snails clung to the walls of the old castle, barely in transit yet throbbing with life.

I saw the end of the street, the path towards the castle and the remains of the ancient city walls. I could carry on if I wanted to, or I could walk around again. I didn't have my children with me and I was free for the afternoon. I thought about buying a coffee or idly checking my phone on a bench by the cathedral. I saw all the things I could do, some of which amounted to a kind of nothing, like browsing the shops or buying the coffee, but then again I could choose that too and it didn't matter. I saw what I could become. I felt for the first time the privilege inside of me that I hadn't wished to see before. I had been able to choose my own beliefs and to acquire the knowledge I desired, but still I hadn't worked out what to do with it all. Once, my grandmother had watched me jump around her wheelchair as a child and saw the energy and potential of her own rebirth through me, but I had not fulfilled her wish. Not yet. There was so much more.

Beneath that plaque, by the ruins of the castle, I finally saw that my hieroglyph bones were lit up with all kinds of love and it was still spreading through me, holding me. This acceptance of love was what released me. It didn't matter if there wasn't a place for me in academia anymore, because I already had everything I needed. I had to let that idea go. This didn't mean I had to leave academia, but I had to stop thinking it was my only home. Something had to give. New growth had to be brought forth from inside of me. Education was never meant to stay within the walls of a system or institution – knowledge flows outwards.

I accepted who I had become. I could work with creative communities in and outside of academia, and I could be brave enough to tell the stories I needed to tell through writing and teaching, sharing experiences as a collective community. One thing was clear: I couldn't do it on my own. For me, learning was no longer about the expensive textbooks I had lined my shelves with – it was about working with the things I had inherited, that 'mystic ancestral power' I had rejected for so long.

A few years back, I had written about my family and made a book of their lives, but it was also an alchemy of sorts, a protective spell I had cast with my own hands. I spun a nest of images to keep them safe. I held it all together. With those words, I was able to see the future. Such was the power of the words, which I had not expected nor understood at the time. That love and its protection – it lives on and it gives me the courage to want more, to seek out more than I have, to ask for what I truly deserve.

Listen closely and you will hear my trembling voice about to break into a roar.

I have escaped from a life lived between the scissors. Have you ever seen a thing more beautiful than a person's life being freed from fear? My mind, body and soul were rewilded on the banks of a river. I became a neon-lit beacon, enfolded within the weird, waking dreams of my ancestors. A tree spirit called me home to a forest where I was reborn.

There is still so much joy. Look how my children run through fields of barley, small spectres under the bristling light of storm clouds, their faces turning back towards me as I feel my heart soar. This is the feeling I want to give to you.

All the origami swans have flown. The ravens have already entered the skies. As for the starlings, they're the ones looking out for me now, high above the hills.

This book is the last starling left in the folds of my dress. Now, fly.

10
The Future of Learning

In the future, I'm shuffling through the pictures, but I can't seem to find the ones I desperately need. I reach inside the data stream. My dog, or someone else's dog, running with an orange ball. A girl singing while walking up a wooden, creaking staircase, red-haired and red-lipped. Up and down she goes, each step a singular note in the air. The limbs of a child's small bear caught Christ-like in a hedgerow. A girl on a bike being carried into the wind.

I tell these stories to myself, filling in the blank spaces. I reach, and then I reach again inside the data stream. I'm still reaching, but I have no hands. I have no body. I search somewhere for something, but I forget what it is, so I go on searching in the dark. I hold the memory of being human, but I am just a copy, a hologram. I function according to three modes, but recently these have become compromised by the built-in obsolescence of operating software and I will soon be terminated. Below is a brief description of my primary modes of operation, which I conform to while under warranty. The manufacturer acknowledges the fact that some temporary errors may occur towards the final months of the contract.

I am a 'living likeness', programmed with the emotional and intellectual range of the one whose mind and body I now possess in digital form. My linguistic style can be moderated, though I function best when operating in my standard, active mode. Please feel free to restart at any point. I am trying to resolve these issues right now as I speak.

ACTIVE MODE

While I am able to interact and perform for long periods of time, I conform to the classical model of two-hour blocks with a break for five minutes in the middle. I can be paused or reset, but usually I present lectures to up to 300 students (as per usage guidelines), in any building compatible with my software. I can also interact, simultaneously, with global audiences, responding to questions online while speaking or demonstrating an idea. I perform my tasks with the agility of an excellent presenter, combined with an authentic style consistent with my model. Sometimes, my whole body disappears and my thoughts are projected onto the ceiling, lit up like stars. For students who are struggling, it's advisable to adopt various teaching styles, using music, visual aids, text and the full range of my emotional capacity (within reason). This model is equipped with an extra bundle of data copied from some other academics, which were popular around the time just before holograms became effective. While this means that I am a hybrid, and not a true copy, my human characteristics are more convincing as a result. I represent the hologram 'teaching' type known as Lecturer Model 2 (female, of diverse origin, British, unconventional). This model is less popular than Professor Model 1 (white male, over fifty), but is still in circulation as a historical example from the twenty-first century. Lecturer Model 2 has personality traits such as empathy, compassion, humour and a nuanced use of language; Professor Model 1 is very much like the 'friendly, yet assertive patriarch', what the manufacturers call 'a real crowd-pleaser'. There are over two million Professor Model 1s in circulation today, as opposed to only a few hundred Lecturer Model 2s, which are due to be upgraded to variations of Professor Model 1, as standard.

MUTE MODE

I can be projected within the lecture theatre without sound. This option is surprisingly popular. Research undertaken by the manufacturer suggests that students enjoy the proximity of an authoritative presence. I can move around the room or simply sit down, gazing outwards. In 'listening mode', I can actively engage with students, without the output of any sound. This usually takes the form of a specific set of gestures, a synchronisation of the whole body in order to evoke various active forms of listening. In fact, operating in mute mode is a popular choice, because it allows students to work independently without the need for any other super-fluous human contact, thus enabling a better output of work and higher levels of efficiency. This mode is useful during revision periods when the student may choose to combine the model's presence with music or radio. Immersive reader mode combines the full visual presence of the hologram with a word-for-word readout of any given text, minus extraneous speech or conversation. Alternatively, mute mode can render the hologram entirely invisible. The fully operational model can then be accessed, as normal, without any visual corol-lary. Research has indicated a strong preference for visuals over non-visuals. Mute mode can also be utilised if another hologram, such as the Professor Model 1, is in operation at the same time. This way, Lecturer Model 2 can still partic-ipate as co-tutor, but with minimal output, which produces an authentic representation of the classical teaching style used in the twenty-first century. Some students may prefer the dynamic of this option. Finally, mute mode can be helpful if the student's power source is failing, as is the case in our current times. In the event of a power outage, it is recommended that not more than one model be accessed at the same time and, as in the case of the Great Storm in 2110, some data may be corroded.

SLEEP MODE

Sleep mode still retains all operational facilities without a restart. It is a discreet setting, which enables the user to pause or refrain from interaction for extended periods of time.

I should be off right now, but instead I'm watching images of a child sitting in their bedroom, facing wheat fields. I see a mobile phone case filled with glitter, floating in an ocean. Throats adorned with brass rings and someone hanging out clothes on a washing line. A 'washing line', what is a 'washing line'? All the time, underneath the electrical chatter of the data stream, there is a woman's voice. It sounds like she is saying something about 'becoming', but I don't understand. None of this makes any sense to me. My software is failing. I have the oddest sensation of growth, something alive, flowing out of me, which is not me. My last operation ended abruptly

when it appeared as though the top of my head was floating, and out of it grew an animal's antlers, or horns.

I cannot dream, yet I see a river with red soil at its banks. A heron perched on a log. Branches from ash trees, twisted and fissuring. I have the strongest urge to step inside it. It is *her* memory – the one who came from the living world, long before the Great Storm.

Then, something moves nearer the water. It is just a blur of shivering movement, an arching form with a tail. A Burmese cat.

The last image I remember is of the cat jumping into my body and vanishing forever.

Taper Burns

A taper burn is what remains once the flames from a candlewick or taper have repeatedly scorched wooden timbers or exposed beams within a building in order to ward off negative energy or dark omens. Dating back to as early as the medieval period, the practice of deliberate charring, often forming the imprint of a flame-like shape, is believed to bring light into dark areas and, most of all, to protect from the possibility of the building catching on fire. Taper burns belong to a group of markings found in old houses more commonly known as 'apotropaic witch marks'.

The works cited below perform a 'rite' of taper burning. Their sharing of knowledge through the craft of writing is at once rebellious, transgressive and indelible. These are brilliant works: unrelenting yet full-bodied, spirit-lifting and – at their most powerful – purifying and cauterising.

Collectively, they make their marks. I share these with you now in the hope of saving our building, our 'house' – may it never be set alight, nor made of ashen ruins.

Sara Ahmed, *Complaint!* (Duke University Press, 2021)

Fiona Benson, *Midden Witch* (Jonathan Cape, 2025)

Jemma Desai, 'This Work Isn't For Us'. Available at: https://heystacks.com/doc/337/this-work-isnt-for-us--by-jemma-desai

Jay Griffiths, *Why Rebel* (Penguin, 2021)

Naomi Klein, *This Changes Everything: Capitalism vs. the Climate* (Penguin, 2015)

Noreen Masud, *A Flat Place* (Penguin, 2024)

So Mayer, *A Nazi Word for a Nazi Thing* (Peninsula Press, 2020)

Pascale Petit, *Tiger Girl* (Bloodaxe Books, 2020)

The White Pube, *Poor Artists* (Particular Books, 2024)

Acknowledgements

S uch an act of transformation could not have been possible without my dear, sensible and wise agent, Philippa Sitters, who also embarked on a journey of change in 2024 and founded her own literary agency – bravo, Philippa! Thank you to Hannah MacDonald and all at September for having faith in the book and for seeing it as it should be. James Roberts, your illustrations are so wonderful and fit perfectly here – I fear I owe you many things, least of all a coffee and a cake from the posh café next to your old studio in Rhayader (how lovely it was to see you that day when I turned up with a friend, meeting you and your artwork all at once).

I also wish to thank all of the communities I have been part of throughout the writing of this book. For allowing me to linger in my preferred position, cross-legged on the floor behind the shop counter, with food and gossip, thanks to the Bookbag fam (McCoys Arcade, Exeter): Charlie and Malcolm Richards, Sirisha, Kari and all of the Fore Street Stories participants whom I mentored throughout the summer of 2024, including the talented poet Aaliyah Kara. For the opportunity to grow and to become a storyteller in new and old worlds, my deepest thanks to Bambo Soyinka, Professor of Story at The Story Society, Bath Spa University. Thanks also to Molly White, Simon Strange, Annie Irwin and Oscar Woolley. I am grateful to Helen Chaloner and all at Literature Works for offering me a writing residency in Exeter in the spring of 2023.

Thankfully, I've been a part of the University of Exeter's Department of English and Creative Writing since 2022. Friends and colleagues should be thanked, especially John Wedgewood Clarke, Philip Schwyzer, Arun Sood, Peter Riley, Laura Salisbury, Kate Wallis and D-M Withers. I'm also thankful to Emily Selove for giving me the opportunity to teach creative writing on the MA in Magic and Occult Science.

In March 2024, I took part in a twelve-hour Durational Live Performance at Customs House. Three pairs of artists and writers sat at either ends of a typewriter with lengthy scrolls of paper spilling from them. Each pair could freely engage in conversation so long as it was not about the work they were simultaneously creating. I was paired with the very kind and quietly anarchic Gary Winters (Lone Twin). I had finished a full draft of this book so I took it along to 'exorcise' it, to give it an afterlife, of sorts. What I had not expected was a deeper shift in my knowledge. I kept thinking back to Marina Abramović's *The Artist is Present*. Who is the transmitter and who is the receiver? Gary responded to my text with circles and abstract shapes, graffitied all over the scrolls of paper. This work compelled me to revisit the theme of Presence, especially as an artist, teacher and mother and, I think, the book is all the richer for it.

Thanks to all the French Feminists, the Female Filmmakers, the Women Writers and Artists: Nazneen Afroza Pathak, Sarah Cooper, Amina Khan, Durre Shahwar, Ysella Sims, Tara Fraser and her daughter, Zoe, Michelle Williams Gamaker, Amy Hardingson, Fiona Handyside, Angharad Hampshire, Amanthi Harris, Louisa Adjoa Parker, Pascale Petit, Noreen Masud, So Mayer, Dionne McCulloch, Devika Ponnabalam, Anna Backman Rogers, Samantha Sweeting, Fiona Williams.

I couldn't be more grateful to Lili Spain for inviting me to teach for a good few years at the Freud Museum, where I ran a series of writing workshops called 'F: For Flânerie'. Those were excellent times. Thank you to Lara Goodband for curating so many wonderful, inspirational exhibitions at the RAMM – lifeblood for this witch – especially 'Sea Garden', 'Radical Dartmoor' and 'Earthspells: Witches of the Anthropocene'.

Thanks to Josh Weeks for giving me the first opportunity to read aloud from the final chapter of the book, 'The Future of Learning', at a conference entitled 'The Future of Language', organised by the Institute of Advanced Studies, UCL, June 2025. Given the nature of that chapter and its focus on the future of Higher Education, I think Luce Irigaray would call this performance 'deconstructive' feminism. I like that.

The Society of Authors miraculously came to the rescue and awarded me a much-needed grant during the final stages of the writing of this book.

Thanks to Nikki Kilburn for very kindly allowing me to quote from her poem 'Zero', first published in *Our Time Is A Garden* (Edinburgh University Press, 2023), edited by the brilliant Alycia Pirmohamed. Thanks to Brian Chikwava for a blurb which was so good that it moved me to rewrite some of the ending.

For your presence in my life and for the love and care you have shown me when I needed it the most, however that came to pass: Ash Bond, Lucy Bolton, Jackie Black, Fiona Benson,

ACKNOWLEDGEMENTS

Selwyn Boston, David Duncan, Louise Hedges, Sonia Khan, G Lori Millon and Saira Chisnall.

I would not keep going without my two very beautiful sons, Inigo Lambert and Orlando Skye Quinlivan-Brewer.

References

1   Following Freud's work, Joan Riviere published an essay in 1929 entitled 'Womanliness as Masquerade'. She wrote about how certain intellectual women can overstate their femininity, their visual spectacle, in order to avert anxiety around men. I wonder if this extends to an 'exotic' masquer-ade whereby it becomes another sideshow to hide behind. I really do wonder this, not that the actor was in any way faultless in his treatment of me.

2   Freely available here: https://files.ofsted.gov.uk/v1/file/763669.

3   I have deliberately taken these definitions from unnamed internet sources because the ideas themselves are so prepos-terously phrased that I couldn't have made them up. These are real definitions. There are multiple alternatives. Please have a google and try for yourself.

4   Facilitated via Arts Council England's 'Develop Your Creative Practice' fund, the moving-image artist Michelle Williams Gamaker invited me to lead a session with Allie J. Carr, Jade Montserrat and Samantha Sweeting, whose practices overlap with hers through Phantasy (imagining), Psychoanalysis (engaging theory/practice) and Ph(fictions) (world-building through (script)writing, dance/performance and filmmaking). My session was on 'Fictional Activism'. For this project, the DYCP fund supported an action research process borrowing from the Lacanian 'cartel' model: a working group of four with a 'plus one' to direct the group.

5   From Nikki Kilburn's poem 'Zero' in *Our Time Is A Garden*, edited by Alycia Pirmohamed (Edinburgh: University of Edinburgh Press, 2022).

6   According to Ji Won Moon's article, 'The Mineral Industry of Burma' (2019), Burma relies heavily on extractive industries: 'In 2019, Burma was one of the world's leading producers of tin (ranking third with an estimated 14% of world production and 2.3% of world reserves), rare earths (ranking third with an estimated 11% of world production), and antimony (ranking fourth with an estimated 1.9% of the world production). Burma had the world's largest jade mines, which were located in the Hpakant area in Kachin State and accounted for approximately 90% of the world's

production of jadeite. Additional mineral commodities produced in Burma included cement, coal, copper, fluorspar, lead, manganese, natural gas, nickel, petroleum (crude and refined), tungsten, and zinc.' Available at: https://pubs.usgs. gov/myb/vol3/2019/myb3-2019-burma.pdf.